# 21
## DAYS OF
# PRAYER

### RELEASING THE SUPERNATURAL
### through the WORD OF GOD

DR. LA TOSHIA PALMER

WESTBOW
PRESS®
A DIVISION OF THOMAS NELSON
& ZONDERVAN

This book is a work of non-fiction. Unless otherwise noted, the author and the publisher
make no explicit guarantees as to the accuracy of the information contained in this book
and in some cases, names of people and places have been altered to protect their privacy.

WestBow Press books may be ordered through booksellers or by contacting:

WestBow Press
A Division of Thomas Nelson & Zondervan
1663 Liberty Drive
Bloomington, IN 47403
www.westbowpress.com
844-714-3454

Because of the dynamic nature of the Internet, any web addresses or links contained in
this book may have changed since publication and may no longer be valid. The views
expressed in this work are solely those of the author and do not necessarily reflect the
views of the publisher, and the publisher hereby disclaims any responsibility for them.

Any people depicted in stock imagery provided by Getty Images are models,
and such images are being used for illustrative purposes only.
Certain stock imagery © Getty Images.

Scriptures are taken from the Holy Bible, New Living Translation, copyright ©
1996, 2004, 2015 by Tyndale House Foundation. Used by permission of Tyndale
House Publishers Inc., Carol Stream, Illinois 60188. All rights reserved.

Scriptures are from the Good News Translation in Today's English Version- Second
Edition Copyright © 1992 by American Bible Society. Used by Permission.

ISBN: 978-1-6642-8825-6 (sc)
ISBN: 978-1-6642-8826-3 (hc)
ISBN: 978-1-6642-8827-0 (e)

Library of Congress Control Number: 2023920284

Print information available on the last page.

WestBow Press rev. date: 11/08/2023

# NOTE

In the beginning was the Word, and the Word was with God, and the Word was God.
—John 1:1

First and foremost, to Almighty God, my Lord and Savior Jesus Christ, and my Helper who teaches me all things—the Holy Spirit. For it is God who works in me both to will and to do for His good pleasure (Philippians 2:13).

To every born-again believer in the faith and to every intercessory prayer warrior, this book is also dedicated to you.

To my family. May it continue to be a legacy and monument of your victory and faith in Christ Jesus!

"He who pays attention to the word (of God), will find good, And blessed (happy, prosperous, to be admired) is he who trusts [confidently] in the LORD" (Proverbs 16:20).

May God continue to bless you and prosper you in all of your ways as you hear, trust, and obey the Word of the Lord! In Jesus's name. Amen.

# CONTENTS

# INTRODUCTION

The purpose of this book is to help you build a strong and solid foundation in prayer. The Lord wants to do a mighty work in your life. He wants you to experience His supernatural presence and the manifestation of His written and Rhema Word in your life by the Holy Spirit—Jesus unlimited. As you grow and strengthen your relationship with Him by studying the Word of God, meditating on the Word of God, feasting on the Word of God, rehearsing the Word of God, decreeing the Word of God, and declaring the Word of God, your faith and confidence in God's Word will be strengthened. In addition, your understanding of the very true essence of His nature and eternal being will be enlightened.

The supernatural power of God is experienced when you become saved and filled with the Holy Spirit and when you believe and have faith in God to perform His Word in your life. When you release the supernatural power of God's Holy Spirit in your life by praying, decreeing, and declaring the Word of God, the name of Jesus will be exalted, miracles will happen, repentance will take place, and people will be brought into a new way of life, which is salvation through Jesus Christ.

*21 Days of Prayer* is not just for you. It is for your family, children, marriage, finances, business, ministry, this world, all nations and countries, and all people in need and who are facing times of distress. *21 Days of Prayer* can be used more than the number of days indicated. You can read, decree, declare, and pray it over and over again and within any format the Holy Spirit leads you to.

When Daniel prayed for 21 days, he presented his supplication before the Lord. Daniel prayed and interceded for his people, the Israelites. When Daniel prayed, he repented on behalf of his people to God for their sins and sought the Lord for forgiveness. Daniel did not come to God in prayer in his own account, but on the account of God and His great compassion (Daniel 9:1–19).

Throughout Daniel's 21 days of prayer, he also fasted and declared the Word of God verbatim. In Daniel 9:4, when he prayed, he confessed the Word of God that was written in Deuteronomy 7:9. Daniel said, "I prayed to the LORD my God and confessed: 'Lord, the great and awesome God, who keeps his covenant of love with those who love him and keep his commandments'" (Daniel 9:4).

It was during these 21 days that Daniel received a breakthrough, vision, prophecy, answered prayer, and revelation knowledge about the coming of the Messiah and the things to come in the end-time (Daniel 9:1–27; Daniel 10–12). All of those things Daniel experienced were out of the ordinary and unusual and transcended the laws of nature. It was a prime example of the supernatural power of God operating in Daniel's life because of his obedience, faith in God, the Word of God, and his time in prayer and fasting.

As you are led by the Holy Spirit, you can fast in addition to your 21 days of prayer (Matthew 4:1–11; Mark 9:29). Daniel said, "So I gave my attention to the Lord God to seek Him by prayer and supplications, with fasting, sackcloth and ashes" (Daniel 9:3). There are four key benefits to fasting and prayer. First, it humbles us and crucifies our flesh. Second, it brings forth spiritual growth. Third, it produces breakthroughs, healing, deliverance, miracles, victory, and blessings. Fourth, it allows us to be more sensitive to the Holy Spirit and so much more! Nevertheless, fasting and prayer do not change God's mind; they change you and encourage you to get closer to God and focused on His Word.

> But the Helper (Comforter, Advocate, Intercessor—Counselor, Strengthener, Standby), the Holy Spirit, whom the Father will send in My name [in My place, to represent Me and act on My behalf], He will teach you all things. And He will help you remember everything that I have told you. (John 14:26)

The Holy Spirit wants His Word to dwell in you richly with all wisdom (Colossians 3:16). He wants you to be so full of His Word that you know how to release His Word on all occasions. He wants you to be ready in season and out of season, to supernaturally release His glory, presence, authority, judgment, and blessings. Through His Word, He wants to use you to bring forth salvation, healing, deliverance, miracles, signs, and wonders. The Holy

Spirit wants to empower you to prophetically release His Word for edification, exhortation, and comfort, to equip the saints for works of ministry and to build up the body of Christ until we all reach unity in the faith and in the knowledge of the Son of God (1 Corinthians 4:3; Ephesians 4:12–13).

# OVERVIEW

Our Father in heaven, hallowed be your name, your kingdom come,
your will be done, on earth as it is in heaven. Give us today our daily
bread. And forgive us our debts as we also have forgiven our debtors.
And lead us not into temptation, but deliver us from the evil one. For
yours is the kingdom and the power and the glory forever. Amen.
—Matthew 6:9–13

The true model for prayer that Jesus provides for us is found in Matthew
6:9–13. Some refer to this as the ACTS framework for prayer, which stands
for adoration, confession, thanksgiving, and supplication. In this case, as you
take time to pray, including the ACTS framework during your prayer time is
a great concept, but it's also important for you to truly understand all that it
entails so that you are not misguided in your growth and maturity as a born-
again believer when you engage in prayer.

## ADORATION, CONFESSION, THANKSGIVING, AND SUPPLICATION (ACTS)

*Adoration* consists of worshiping God for who He is and telling Him how
wonderful He is. Our adoration for God should be the first thing we do as
we engage in prayer. When this happens, we take time to set the atmosphere
for Jesus to be exalted and for the presence of God and the Holy Spirit to
empower us to accomplish His will through us in prayer. There are various
examples of adoration in the Bible. As an example, some are found in the
following scriptures:

The LORD reigns, He is clothed with majesty. The LORD
has clothed and girded Himself with strength; Indeed, the

world is firmly established, it will not be moved. Your throne is established from of old; You are from everlasting. (Psalm 93:1–2)

Exalt the LORD our God And worship at His footstool; Holy is He. (Psalm 99:5)

Worthy are You, our Lord and our God, to receive glory and honor and power; for You created all things, and because of Your will they existed, and were created. (Revelation 4:11)

*Confession.* As the Holy Spirit leads you, take time to talk to God about where you made a mistake, admitting your sin and asking God to restore your relationship with Jesus Christ. When this happens, God displays His forgiveness, unconditional love, mercy, and grace toward you and brings you back into right standing and fellowship with Him (1 John 1:9). This is one particular topic of discussion that cannot be briefly covered.

Let's talk a little bit more about confession of sin. As born-again believers, and specifically for those who are new babes in Christ, we need to understand that Jesus will perfect everything concerning us until He returns (Psalms 138:8; Romans 8:28). However, that does not mean that we keep on sinning and missing the mark intentionally because we know that if we confess our sins and ask God for forgiveness, He will grant it. If this is happening in our lives, it's primarily because we have not been delivered from our old adamic nature that caused us to fall into deception, which is the root cause of *sin* and its evil fruits of destruction, which are the works of the flesh *sins* (Galatians 5:19–21).

Watchman Nee provides us with a vivid example of what some of us may have been going through:

> When God's light first shines into my heart, my one cry is forgiveness, for I realize I have committed *sins* before him; but when, once I have received forgiveness of sins, I make a new discovery, namely, the discovery of *sin,* and I realize not only that I have committed sins before God, but that there is something wrong within. I discovered that I have the nature of a sinner. There is an inward inclination to sin, a power within that draws to sin. When that power breaks out, I

commit sins. I may seek and receive forgiveness, but then I sin once more. So life goes on a vicious circle of sinning and being forgiven and then sinning again. I appreciate the blessed fact of God's forgiveness, but I want something more than that: I want deliverance. I need forgiveness for what I have done, but I need also deliverance from what I am. (Nee 1961)

In the Bible, Paul provides us with a vivid example of what some of may be going through as well:

For what I am doing, I do not understand; for I am not practicing what I would like to do, but I am doing the very thing I hate. But if I do the very thing I do not want to do, I agree with the Law, confessing that the Law is good. So now, no longer I am the one doing it, but sin which dwells in me. For I know that nothing good dwells in me, that is my flesh; for the willing is present in me but the doing of the good is not. For the good that I want, I do not do, but I practice the very evil that I do not want. But if I am doing the very thing I do not want, I am no longer the one doing it, but sin which dwells in me. I find then the principle that evil is present in me, the one who wants to do good. For I joyfully concur with the law of God in the inner man, but I see a different law in the members of my body, waging war against the law of my mind and making me a prisoner of the law of sin which is in my members. Wretched man that I am! Who will set me free from the body of this death? Thanks be unto God through Jesus Christ our Lord. So on the other hand, I myself with my mind am serving the law of God, but on the other, with my flesh the law of sin. (Romans 7:15–25)

Watchman Nee and apostle Paul understood what it was like to deal with the war going on inside of them. They were saved, wanted to do good, did good, fell short and repented, received forgiveness, and then felt short again. They both came to the realization that they needed to be delivered from sinning and that this was something they could not do on their own. They needed to renew their minds. Continuing to practice sin knowing that you have been given a free grace pass is deception. It is a lie and trick of the enemy. Sin separates man from God, and the Bible says that the wage of sin is death (in the natural and spiritual). Let's take a look at Romans 6:1–14:

> What shall we say, then? Shall we go on sinning so that grace may increase? By no means! We are those who have died to sin; how can we live in it any longer? Or don't you know that all of us who were baptized into Christ Jesus were baptized into his death? We were therefore buried with him through baptism into death in order that, just as Christ was raised from the dead through the glory of the Father, we too may live a new life. For if we have been united with him in a death like his, we will certainly also be united with him in a resurrection like his. For we know that our old self was crucified with him so that the body ruled by sin might be done away with, that we should no longer be slaves to sin—because anyone who has died has been set free from sin. Now if we died with Christ, we believe that we will also live with him. For we know that since Christ was raised from the dead, he cannot die again; death no longer has mastery over him. The death he died, he died to sin once for all; but the life he lives, he lives to God. In the same way, count yourselves dead to sin but alive to God in Christ Jesus. Therefore do not let sin reign in your mortal body so that you obey its evil desires. Do not offer any part of yourself to sin as an instrument of wickedness, but rather offer yourselves to God as those who have been brought from death to life; and offer every part of yourself to him as an instrument of righteousness. For sin shall no longer be your master, because you are not under the law, but under grace.

It's important to understand that as born-again believers, we are living underneath a new dispensation of God's mercy and grace. Therefore, the solution for being delivered—putting to death the deeds of the body from our old adamic nature and from the waging war between our flesh and our spirit—is found in the blood of Jesus, the cross, and renewing our minds, coming into a full understanding of who we are in Christ. The blood of Jesus Christ that was shed for us at the cross was the perfect atonement. The blood of Jesus completely eradicates our sins and cleanses us from an evil conscience so that we can approach God boldly and in confidence, based on the finished works of Christ. Therefore, The blood of Jesus gives us access to the Father in prayer; it severs the mental accusations of the enemy, and it makes us justified in Christ Jesus (Romans 3:24–26; Hebrews 10:22; Ephesians 2:13; Romans 4:8; Hebrews 9:11–14).

"Our old history ends with the Cross and our new history begins with the resurrection" (Nee 1957). The cross that Jesus Christ died on for us on Calvary deals with the root cause of our capacity to sin and represents our new nature in Christ. When Christ died on the cross, God thought about us, that we too might die from our old, sinful (adamic) nature. According to 2 Corinthians 5:14, one died for all, and then all died. Galatians 2:20 also says, "I have been crucified with Christ; it is no longer I who live, but Christ lives in me; and the *life* which I now live in the flesh I live by faith in the Son of God, who loved me and gave Himself for me." Therefore, as born-again believers, since we are now dead and buried in Christ, we are no longer in bondage to sin. The resurrection of Christ makes all things new, and from this we learn to put on the new man according to Colossians 3:1–17, because we are justified in Christ Jesus.

This is who we are in Christ. We are redeemed and justified. The works of Jesus Christ dying on the cross for our sins redeemed us and set us free from the bondage of sin and death. We have been called to live a justified life in Christ Jesus. A life that represents the true nature and character of Jesus Christ. We are the righteousness of God in Christ Jesus, and we are to practice exactly that on a daily basis (2 Corinthians 5:21). Once born again, you are made alive by the Spirit of God, and if the Spirit of God dwells in you, then you will not have a desire for the lust of the flesh or to walk in the flesh but to walk in the spirit (Galatians 2:20).

The purpose for our confession to God about our sins exists to remind us about the importance of examining ourselves daily—not to beat people over their heads because of their sins and shortcomings. No one is perfect! Living a life that is holy and consecrated before God takes time because, as Christians, everyone is working out their own salvation (Philippians 2:12). We are all in different stages in our walk with Christ. Keeping ourselves pure is not an easy task, and there is no way for us to do this in our own strength. We need the Holy Spirit / God's help and His grace in order to become more like Him each and every day (Hebrews 4:16). This is why it's so important for us to examine ourselves daily.

Our confession allows us to take time to examine ourselves so that we don't stunt our growth as believers. Furthermore, it provides us the opportunity to dismantle the spirits of strife and pride so that our relationships can be restored, so that our churches can grow and operate in the full power and the anointing of the ministry gifts of the Holy Ghost, so that our prayers will be heard and not hindered, so that we may receive our healing and deliverance, and, most important, so that we will not grieve the Holy Spirit (James 5:14–16; Mark 11:25; James 3:16; 1 Corinthians 1:10; Ephesians 4:29–32).

God wants us to do our best to represent Him well by demonstrating His character to produce good fruit (Galatians 5:22–26). He wants our lights to shine so much that others will be drawn to Jesus as a result of His presence illuminating from the inside of us. Some questions to consider as we examine ourselves may consist of the following:

- Am I walking in the flesh or in the spirit (Galatians 5:16)?
- Did I miss the mark on this matter (2 Corinthians 2:10–11)?
- Did I misjudge my brother or sister in Christ (Matthew 7:1; Luke 6:37; Luke 6:41; John 8:7; Romans 2:1; Romans 14:10; Romans 14:13; 1 Corinthians 4:5)?
- Am I offended or angry by my brother or sister, husband, wife, child, boss, neighbor, or someone else (Ephesians 4:26; Matthew 18:15–17)?
- Did I partially or fully obey God in this situation (Acts 5:29; 1 Samuel 15:1–27)?
- Am I trying to fit in (John 17:16)?

For these reasons, an example of how one can make a confession unto God is provided for your use within the ACTS framework. It is not intended to hold anyone to self-condemnation. The Bible says that there is no self-condemnation to those who are in Christ Jesus (Romans 8:1). As Christians, we are expected to strive for perfection-holiness until the day of Christ Jesus (Ephesians 4:13–14; Titus 2:11–14; Hebrews 6:1; 1 Peter 1:15–16). God expects us to move beyond the stages of being babes in Christ (1 Corinthians 3:2–3). He wants us to become mature believers in Christ, full of the Holy Ghost, who are forever growing and increasing in wisdom, stature, and favor with God and man (Luke 2:52; Romans 12:1–2; Hebrews 5:14; Hebrews 6:1–2). This means we are to do our utmost to live at peace with all and to live a life that demonstrates our obedience to God's Word at all times (Hebrews

12:14; Galatians 5:18–25). As we continue to do this on a daily basis, we are positioning ourselves to release the supernatural!

*Thanksgiving.* Thanksgiving requires giving total praise unto God for the things that He has done in your life. Take time to thank Him for his mercy, grace, and loving-kindness. Having a thankful heart can change your perspective of your situation. It will take your mind off your problems and shift your focus toward the promises and blessing of God. When you start to give thanks to God in all things, your faith will grow, and you will begin to experience God move in your life (Psalm 107:1–3).

*Supplication.* Supplication entails earnestly seeking God for Him to do something on our behalf or for someone else, with an expectation that He will do it. According to *Webster's Revised Unabridged Dictionary*, it also means to make a humble petition, an earnest request or entreaty. In this book, you will find supplication as the main title over every prayer, declaration, and decree. Philippians 4:6 tells us, "Be anxious for nothing, but in everything by prayer and supplication, with thanksgiving, let your requests be made known to God."

## In the Name of Jesus

Throughout this book, you will find within each prayer, decree, and declaration the emphasis of "In the name of Jesus." According to scripture, there are several reasons why this exists. Listed below are several examples of why "in the name of Jesus" occurs:

- The name of Jesus is above all names (Philippians 2:9).
- Jesus is our advocate, intercessor, and power of attorney. The name of Jesus gives us access to the Father (Romans 8:34; Hebrews 4:16; 1 John 2:1).
- We have a legal right and the authority to use the name of Jesus to do all that God has called us to do (Colossians 3:17).
- The name of Jesus gives us power over devils (Mark 16:17–18).
- We are justified in the name of Jesus (1 Corinthians 6:11).
- We are baptized in the name of Jesus (Acts 2:38; Matthew 28:19).

Last, it is important to state that using "in the name of Jesus" is not a catch-all phrase; nor is it used to make something majestically happen. This type of example is not the foundation of prayer, decrees, or declarations. To do so is not biblical and is not supported by scripture. Anyone who calls themself a Christian and practices such foolishness of wickedness, witchcraft, and sorcery is in error and subject to the judgment of God (Matthew 7:22; 2 Timothy 3:8; Acts 8:9–24; Acts 19:11–20).

## CONCLUSION

As you go through each day of this book, following supplications you will find either a prayer, decree, or declaration for your use. Every prayer, decree, and declaration provided has been strategically designed to cover a certain topic or situation the Holy Spirit directed me to share with you for each day. At the end of each day, you are provided with the opportunity to personalize your own prayer, decree, or declaration.

# The Significance of Prayer, Decrees, and Declarations

## Prayer

Prayer is faith-based communication between God and man. It involves a process that requires faith and an exchange of talking and listening—you talking and listening to God, and God talking and listening to you (1 John 5:14). It also involves you asking God to grant your request according to His Word. During this exchange of reciprocal communication and requests, a level of intimacy and relationship building takes place. Notice that it all begins with faith and communication.

Having faith in God, His Word, His promises, and His communication is important because it constitutes the essential aspects of our prayer language. In order to employ our prayer language, we are required to open our mouths and speak. Through the unction of the Holy Spirit, one can either speak in other tongues (their heavenly prayer language), travail, groan, speak in English, or declare, decree, and make petitions based on the Word of God.

James 5:16 says that the effectual and fervent prayer of the righteous avails much and makes tremendous power available. Daniel prayed three times a day (Daniel 6:10). From this, we can see Daniel's faith and communication with God on a consistent basis. Likewise, we need to make prayer a priority on a consistent basis. This is critical! When you make time to pray and to pray God's Word consistently, on a daily basis, with persistence and unwavering faith, your prayers will prevail. That's the key—faith. Nothing but faith pleases the Father (Hebrews 11:6). Therefore, you have to understand and have faith that God hears you every time you pray and that you have received everything you have asked of God in prayer (1 John 5:15; Mark 11:24). Confessing God's Word during prayer releases our provision, our protection, and our power (2 Corinthians 9:8; 2 Peter 1:13; Job 38:41; John 10:10; Luke

12:7; Psalm 91; Isaiah 54:17; Ephesians 6:13–18; James 5:16). When we pray God's Word, He hastens (to be alert, sleepless, to be on the lookout) to His Word to perform it (Jeremiah 1:12). The Bible also tells us that God's Word does not return to Him void, that it will accomplish what He pleases and that it shall prosper in the thing for which it was sent (Isaiah 55:11).

Before Jesus went out to minister to multitudes of people, He spent time in prayer (Matthew 14:23; Mark 1:35; Luke 5:16, 6:12). Jesus was disciplined and obedient to the ministry of prayer. His obedience in prayer resulted in many miracles, healings, deliverance, and salvation.

Furthermore, prayer is our God-given right and privilege as children of God. Hebrews 4:16 (Ellicott's Commentary) says that we can come boldly (without any doubt or fear, trusting in His sacrifice and intercession for acceptance) to the throne of grace (the throne of our reconciled Father, which grace erected and where it reigns and dispenses all blessings in a way of unmerited favor), so that we may receive mercy (to pardon all our past sins and compassionate our condition amid our various infirmities and sufferings) and find grace to help us in our time of need (a seasonable help according to our respective necessities)—times in which we want supplies of grace. Sometimes are peculiarly as such—seasons of affliction, persecution, and temptation. Or times when God chastises us for our lukewarmness and sloth, our hypocrisy and formality, or pride, self-will, discontent, or impatience.

Now that we have completed a general summary of what prayer is, here is a brief description of what prayer is not:

- optional
- being silent
- not talking
- thinking good thoughts
- praying to the universe
- vain repetition
- exalting oneself
- self-centered

## GOD'S WORD AND HIS RESPONSE TO PRAYER

There are many scriptures about the significance of God's Word, His response to our prayers, and how we are to approach God in prayer. Listed below are several examples evidenced by scripture of what God says specifically about His Word.

> In the beginning was the Word, and the Word was with God, and the Word was God. He was in the beginning with God. All things came into being through Him, and apart from Him nothing came into being that has come into being. In Him was life, and the life was the Light of men. (John 1:1–4)

> All Scripture is God-breathed and is useful for teaching, rebuking, correcting and training in righteousness, so that the servant of God may be thoroughly equipped for every good work. (2 Timothy 3:16)

> For the word of God is alive and active. Sharper than any double-edged sword, it penetrates even to dividing soul and spirit, joints and marrow; it judges the thoughts and attitudes of the heart. (Hebrews 4:12)

> So shall my word be that goeth forth out of my mouth: it shall not return unto me void, but it shall accomplish that which I please, and it shall prosper in the thing whereto I sent it. (Isaiah 55:11)

The Lord is always ready to hear us and forgive us, and He grants our request when we pray. The significance of God's response to our prayer, decrees, and declarations according to the Word of God can be found in the following scriptures:

> Before they call I will answer; while they are still speaking I will hear. (Isaiah 65:24)

> Therefore I tell you, whatever you ask for in prayer, believe that you have received it, and it will be yours. (Mark 11:24)

> Truly, truly, I say to you, he who believes in Me, the works that I do, he will do also; and greater *works* than these he will do; because I go to the Father. Whatever you ask in My

name, that will I do, so that the Father may be glorified in the Son. If you ask Me anything in My name, I will do *it*. (John 14:12–14)

And when you stand praying, if you hold anything against anyone, forgive them, so that your Father in heaven may forgive you your sins. (Mark 11:25)

Thou shalt also decree a thing, and it shall be established unto thee: and the light shall shine upon thy ways. (Job 22:28)

## APPROACHING THE LORD IN PRAYER

Approaching the Lord in prayer should never be complicated because we serve a loving Father. He wants to spend time with us, and He is concerned about what is on our heart. As a child of God, we are to first have faith in God! Jesus said to have faith in God. It is also written in His Word that we should not doubt (Mark 11:22–24). Hebrews 11:6 states, "And without faith it is impossible to please God, because anyone who comes to Him must believe that He exists and that He rewards those who earnestly seek Him."

As we pray the Word of God, decree the Word of God, and declare the Word of God according to His will, we are putting our faith and trust in God alone, who answers prayer—not in our ourselves. In addition, as we approach God in prayer, we are to be humble and have a sincere reverence (a holy fear) for Him and His Word. To be humble and have a reverence for God's Word is so important. There is a level of accountability that God expects us to have according to His Word. Jesus said in John 12:47–48, "If anyone hears my words but does not keep them, I do not judge that person. For I did not come to judge the world, but to save the world. There is a judge for the one who rejects me and does not accept my words; the very words I have spoken will condemn them at the last day."

At the same time, we should be confident, bold, and anxious for nothing when we come before the Lord in prayer. Listed below are scriptures for additional reference:

And this is the boldness which we have toward him, that, if we ask anything according to his will, he heareth us, and if we know that he heareth us whatsoever we ask, we know that we have the petitions which we have asked of him. (1 John 5:14–15)

Let us then approach God's throne of grace with confidence, so that we may receive mercy and find grace to help us in our time of need. (Hebrews 4:16)

Do not be anxious about anything, but in every situation, by prayer and petition, with thanksgiving, present your requests to God. (Philippians 4:6)

And when you pray, do not be like the hypocrites, for they love to pray standing in the synagogues and on the street corners to be seen by others. Truly I tell you, they have received their reward in full. But when you pray, go into your room, close the door and pray to your Father, who is unseen. Then your Father, who sees what is done in secret, will reward you. And when you pray, do not keep on babbling like pagans, for they think they will be heard because of their many words. Do not be like them, for your Father knows what you need before you ask him. (Matthew 6:5–8)

## DECREES

A decree is an official order issued by a legal authority. It is a commandment, law, edict, order, proclamation, and/or mandate. According to the Strong's Concordance, the word for *decree* in Hebrew is ḥōq (H2706). In Greek, a decree is called *dogma* (G1378). Throughout this text, I will use the term *proclamation* in reference to a decree. Jesus is our high priest and legal authority. Jesus gave a decree to the church—the Great Commission. In Matthew 28:18, Jesus said, "All authority in heaven and on earth has been given to me. Therefore go and make disciples of all nations, baptizing them in the name of the Father and of the Son and of the Holy Spirit, and teaching them to obey everything I have commanded you. And surely I am with you always, to the very end of the age."

The decree of the Great Commission does not end until Jesus comes back for us, His church, the Ekklesia. The age cannot come to an end until we have done our job as the church of Jesus Christ, His witnesses on earth, which is to decree (proclaim) the Gospel in all the world and as a witness to all the nations.

Jesus also provided another decree (and within the context of spiritual warfare). He told the devil, it is written, "Man shall not live on bread alone, but on every word that comes out of the mouth of God" (Matthew 4:4).

As you can see, Jesus is the prime example within the context of executing a decree because He is King of kings and Lord of lords. Furthermore, Jesus is our apostle and the high priest of our confession. Hebrews 3:1 says, "Therefore, holy brethren, partakers of the heavenly calling, consider the Apostle and High Priest of our *confession*, Christ Jesus."

Jesus Christ is our confession because He is the truth, the way, and the life. He is the Living Word of God. In John 14:5–7 (AMP), Jesus said to Thomas, "I am the [only] Way [to God] and the [real] Truth and the [real] Life; no one comes to the Father but through Me." According to Romans 10:10, with our mouths, confession is made unto salvation. Therefore, salvation cannot be received unless one confesses with their mouth Jesus Christ is Lord. The scripture says, "If you declare with your mouth, 'Jesus is Lord,' and believe in your heart that God raised him from the dead, you will be saved. For with the heart man believeth unto righteousness; and with the mouth confession is made unto salvation" (Romans 10:9–10 NLT and KJB).

Let's talk about salvation for a moment. Salvation is an important topic of discussion in relation to the context of our confession. Salvation is an all-inclusive word that entails the very inheritance we obtained from the death and crucifixion of our Lord and Savior, Jesus Christ. Jesus died in order for us to have the following:

- the gift of eternal life
- the forgiveness of our sins
- healing in our physical bodies.
- deliverance from demonic forces and influences
- the power of His Holy Spirit to help lead us, guide us, and sustain us

- the ability to utilize our gifts and talents to spread the Gospel (advance the kingdom of God)
- the ability to give and receive blessings—a life full of abundance and prosperity

The opportunity to receive the gift of salvation is available to all humankind throughout the entire world! Have you confessed Jesus Christ is Lord? If you have no confession, then you have no high priest. In order to have a confession, you can pray the prayer of salvation according to Romans 10:9 and within the latter section of this book, titled "Prayer of Salvation." After you have prayed the prayer of salvation and if you are saved and made Jesus Christ your confession, then you now have the right and privilege as His child and ambassador to officially appropriate and confess by faith the written and Rhema Word of God in your life, which entails all of your inheritance! Jesus Christ is our high priest in respect to what we confess. According to Derick Prince, a world-renowned international Bible teacher,

> Whenever we say out of our mouth and whatever the Bible says about us as Believers in Jesus, then we have Jesus as our High Priest in Heaven releasing His authority and blessing. But if we remain silent, we shut off His Ministry as High Priest. Furthermore, if we make a wrong confession-we invite negative forces to surround us and move upon us. Proclamation (decree's) releases the authority of God's Word into a situation that needs the Power of God released into them. Proclaiming (decreeing), is the activity of a herald, a person of authority from a King, duke or nobleman who went to the area of concern and made a proclamation (decree) of the will and the decision of the God of the ruler of that particular place.

We must understand, brothers and sisters in Christ, that we too are heralds. Jesus Christ has given us authority, and God has already given us the power of the Holy Spirit to rule and reign in this life by executing the Word of God (Luke 10:19; Ephesians 1:19–20). As born-again believers, we just need to have the faith to release it. We are preachers and heirs of God and joint heirs of Jesus Christ (Romans 8:17). We are a chosen people, a royal priesthood, a holy nation, a people for God's own possession, so that we may *proclaim* the excellencies (His mercy, grace, loving-kindness, freedom, authority and power, purity and holiness) of the one having called us out of darkness into His marvelous light (1 Peter 2:9).

Jesus commissioned us to preach and decree (proclaim) the will of God, which is the Word of God—the Gospel of Jesus Christ, to the end of age (Matthew 24:14). In addition, according to the Amplified Bible, in Luke 10:19, Jesus said to us, "I have given you authority [that you now possess] to tread on serpents and scorpions, and [the ability to exercise authority] over all the power of the enemy (Satan); and nothing will [in any way] harm you."

With the authority and power that Jesus has given us, we have the right and the privilege to make a decree according to the Word of God—decrees that are righteous and just and are in alignment with the will, plan, and purpose of God and according to the Word of God (Psalm 119:7, 144, 160, and 164). When we make a decree by faith, we should be opening up our mouths and speaking what God has already written and said in His Word. When the words we speak out of our mouth line up and agree with the Word of God, we make ourselves available to receive the full authority and guarantee of Jesus (our advocate and intercessor), to ensure the releasing of God's authority and power into our lives and circumstances in order to execute blessings and judgment according to the Word of God.

> Let the godly ones exult in glory; Let them sing for joy on their beds. *Let* the high praises of God *be* in their mouth, and a two-edged sword in their hand to execute vengeance on the nations, and punishment on the peoples; To bind their kings with chain And their nobles with fetters of iron, To execute on them the judgment written; This is an honor for all His godly ones. Praise the LORD! (Psalm 149:5–9)

By faith, Moses used his rod to execute judgment on Pharaoh and the Egyptians (Exodus 14:15–31). Queen Esther boldly made a decree to help save the Jews. King Ahasuerus said to Queen Esther, "Now write another decree in the king's name in behalf of the Jews as seems best to you, and seal it with the king's signet ring—for no document written in the king's name and sealed with his ring can be revoked" (Esther 8:7–8). As believers, we are expected to decree the written and Rhema Word of God by faith and boldly under the anointing of the Holy Spirit. It is the Spirit of God that ushers the Word of God out of our mouths with the authority and power of God to supernaturally release it into a situation. "Thou shalt also decree a thing, and it shall be established unto thee, and the light shall shine upon thy ways" (Job 22:28).

The word *decree* appears approximately eighty-two times in the Bible. Listed below are several examples for your reference:

> Thou shalt also decree a thing, and it shall be established unto thee: and the light shall shine upon thy ways. (Job 22:28)

> Now write another decree in the king's name in behalf of the Jews as seems best to you, and seal it with the king's signet ring—for no document written in the king's name and sealed with his ring can be revoked. (Esther 8:8)

> In those days Caesar Augustus issued a decree that a census should be taken of the entire Roman world. (Luke 2:1)

> But in the first year of Cyrus king of Babylon, Cyrus the king made a decree to build this house of God. (Ezra 5:13)

## Declare—Declarations

According to Strong's Concordance, the word *declare* in Hebrew is *śîaḥ* (H7878), and it means to meditate, talk, speak, complain, pray, commune, muse, and declare. The word *declare* in Greek is *exēgeomai* (G1834), which means to lead out, make known, rehearse, and declare.

Just as we can make a decree according to the will and Word of God, we can also declare it. Declarations are confessions of our faith based on the Word of God that can be spoken out loud and rehearsed during corporate or individual prayer. That being said, declarations are an integral part of prayer. When we take time to declare the Word of God by faith and with the authority, anointing, and power of God's Holy Spirit over ourselves, children, grandchildren, spouse, marriages, relationships, finances, ministry, church, business, this world and its systems, leaders and governors of authority, individuals in need, people who are going through difficult times, our neighborhoods, cities, regions, nations, countries, and the world, a significant change will take place. The supernatural power of God Almighty Himself will cause His Word to manifest!

If the promises of God have not been manifested in your life or situation, then you need to start declaring it and keep declaring it until it happens. Regardless of how you feel, hear, or see, don't be moved by it. Don't be deceived by the enemy's tactics (distractions, delays, and disappointments). Stay focused! God's timing is always perfect. Declaring the Word of God is not based on your five senses. It is based on the legitimacy of God's Holy Word that has the power and authority to supernaturally intervene and change your situation and circumstance, if and only if you believe it.

I believe the whole Bible and all of the promises of God in it. I will keep on declaring the written and Rhema Word of God concerning a situation in my life and according to His will until it comes to pass. I will call those things that be not as though they were if it has not come to pass yet according to what has already been decreed (proclaimed) in His Word (Romans 4:17). I have full confidence in God Almighty to release His supernatural power and authority of His Word into my life and current situation when I open up my mouth and speak His Word into existence!

There is power of life and death in the tongue, and to this day, I use my tongue as a weapon to release the Word of God (Proverbs 18:21). The Word of God is the sword of the Spirit, and it is a part of the believer's spiritual armor (Ephesians 6:17). Furthermore, God's Word is the final authority in all the affairs of life. Jesus said, "The Words I speak to you, they are Spirit and they are life!" (John 6:63). Better yet, His Word is truth. He does not turn back on His Word. He does exactly what He said He would do according to His Word. According to Numbers 23:19 (GNT), "God is not like people who lie; He is not a human who changes his mind. Whatever he promises, he does; He speaks, and it is done." Let's take a look at Jeremiah 1:11–12:

> And the word of the LORD came to me, asking, "Jeremiah, what do you see?" "See a branch of an almond tree," I replied. "You have observed correctly," said the LORD, "for I am watching over My word to accomplish it."

According to 2 Corinthians 1:20, "For all the promises of God in Him are 'yea'; and in Him 'amen' unto the glory of God by us." When we declare the Word of God by faith, we are rehearsing and speaking forth the promises of God that were already proclaimed since the beginning of time, which was already spoken into existence by God Almighty Himself.

It is important to emphasize that when we make bold declarations according to the Word of God, we are not causing things to mysteriously happen in our own efforts. Nor are we using God's Word and the power of His Holy Spirit to manipulate or control people, circumstances, or situations. And we are not to use the Word of God and the Spirit of God to try to manipulate God to do things for us or for selfish reasons. Trying to buy the gift of God with money, using the church as a means for profit, or claiming to possess supernatural abilities discredits the power of Almighty God and grieves the Holy Spirit. To do so is a sin and is witchcraft. An example of this is found in Acts 8:9–24 regarding Simon the sorcerer, who converted to Christianity but then turned around and tried to offer Peter and John money in order to receive the gift of the Holy Spirit. As Christians, we are not to partake in any such practices of sin. As a reminder, we are a new creation in Christ Jesus. We have been redeemed by the blood and crucified with Christ.

The word *declare* occurs approximately 346 times in the Bible. Listed below are several examples for your reference:

> Let them give glory to the LORD, And declare His praise in the coastlands. (Isaiah 42:12)

> I will set a sign among them; and those among them who escape I will send to the nations: *to* Tarshish and Pul and Lud, who draw the bow, and Tubal and Javan, *to* the coastlands afar off who have not heard My fame nor seen My glory. And they shall declare My glory among the Gentiles. (Isaiah 66:19)

> Sing praises to the LORD, who dwells in Zion! Declare His deeds among the people. (Psalm 9:11)

> For the director of music. A psalm of David. The heavens declare the glory of God; the skies proclaim the work of his hands. (Psalm 19:1)

*Father, in the name of Jesus, let the fire on our altar never burn out. Make us a house of prayer (Matthew 21:13). As Your kings and priest, I pray that we take our positions to rule and reign in prayer. Let every God-breathed Word of God released from our mouth supernaturally transform our life, environment, people, and circumstances for Your glory. I pray in the name of Jesus that the power of God's Holy Spirit will anoint you, sanctify you, and use you as His vessel to bring forth supernatural miracles, signs, and wonders as you pray, decree, and declare the Word of God.*

## Prayer of Salvation

It is imperative for us to be sure that before we engage in prayer, decrees, declarations, or any ministry, we have received the gift of salvation (Romans 10:9). To receive God's gift of salvation, please pray the following prayer of salvation:

> *Father, in the name of Jesus, You said in Your Word that if I confess from my mouth that Jesus is Lord and believe in my heart that God raised Him from the dead, I shall be saved. You also said in Your Word, "For with the heart, man believeth unto righteousness, and with the mouth confession is made unto salvation" (Romans 10:9–10).*
>
> *Because of your infallible and unadulterated Word and because you are a God who cannot lie, I confess with my mouth Jesus is my Lord, and I make Him my Lord and Savior in this very moment. I believe in my heart that You raised Jesus from the dead, and I receive your salvation. I confess my sins and renounce my former life and all ungodly connections with Satan, and I close the door to any and all of his devices.*
>
> *I thank You, Father, for forgiving me of my sins. I thank You that Jesus Christ is my Lord and Savior and that I am a new creation in Christ Jesus (2 Corinthians 5:17). In Jesus's name. Amen.*

Now that you have prayed the prayer of salvation, it is good to obtain water baptism as a symbol and outward expression of your faith, salvation, and separation from the world (Matthew 3:11; Matthew 28:19; John 3:5). Most importantly, it is highly encouraged that you receive the baptism of the Holy Spirit.

# The Baptism of the Holy Spirit

When your heart becomes filled with the Holy Spirit, out of your mouth, the Holy Spirit will speak. When your heart is filled to overflowing, the mouth is in position to speak as the Holy Spirit gives you the words to speak. God is Spirit. God filled them, and the Holy Spirit gave them the language.

All we have to do is position ourselves to receive the Holy Spirit. You can directly receive the Holy Spirit by faith from heaven, or you can receive the Holy Spirit by the laying on of hands. In order to position yourself to receive the baptism of the Holy Spirit and with fire, there are several steps you must take:

1. Repent and confess Jesus Christ as your Lord and Savior. "Peter said to them, Repent, and each of you be baptized in the name of Jesus Christ for the forgiveness of your sins; and you will receive the gift of the Holy Spirit" (Acts 2:38).
2. Be baptized (Acts 2:38).
3. Have a hunger and thirst to be filled.
4. "Blessed are those who hunger and thirst after righteousness, for they shall be filled" (Matthew 5:6).
5. Seek Jesus Christ for the baptism of the Holy Spirit, not man. Man is the vessel of honor, which He uses as a conduit to minister the baptism of the Holy Spirit. Man is not the giver of the Holy Spirit. Jesus is.
6. Ask your heavenly Father for the gift of the Holy Spirit. Luke 11:11–13 says, "Now suppose one of you fathers is asked by his son for a fish; he will not give him a snake instead of a fish, will he? Or if he is asked for an egg, he will not give him a scorpion, will he? If you then, being evil, know how to give good gifts to your children, how

much more will your heavenly Father give the Holy Spirit to those who ask Him?"

7. Receive the gift of the Holy Spirit.

8. Yield and submit your tongue to God. Those who are hungry and thirsty open their mouths to eat and drink. Therefore, you will need to open your mouth and allow the Holy Spirit to take control of your tongue and to give you things to say and do that glorify God and act as evidence that the Holy Spirit is in you (Acts 2:4).

The infilling of the Holy Spirit, combined with the evidence of speaking in tongues, is a New Testament seal and sign (audible and public) that you belong to Christ (1 Corinthians 1:21–22 and Ephesians 1:13–14; Acts 2:4). If you have reviewed the seven steps outlined here, are hungry and thirsty and have the desire to receive the gift of the baptism of the Holy Spirit, by faith in our Lord Jesus Christ, who is the baptizer of the Holy Spirit, pray the following prayer:

## Prayer to Receive the Baptism of the Holy Spirit

*Father, in the name of Jesus, I come before You because I desire to be baptized with Your Holy Spirit with the evidence of speaking in other tongues. Your Word says, according to Luke 11:13, "If you then, being evil, know how to give good gifts to your children, how much more, will your heavenly Father give the Holy Spirit to those who ask Him?" Therefore, I am asking You to baptize me with Your Holy Spirit and fire, with the evidence of speaking in tongues. I declare and decree that I can have it, and I believe what You have said. I receive this gift by faith in Jesus's name. Thank You, Father, that I am baptized with the Holy Spirit with the evidence of speaking in other tongues. In Jesus's name. Amen!*

## DELIVERANCE

## FAVOR

## LOOSING THE WORD OF GOD

### ADORATION

Father, in the name of Jesus, I enter through Your gates with thanksgiving and into Your courts with praise (Psalm 100:4). I am thankful that You are my God and my Father, and I bless Your holy name. I thank You for waking me up this morning and allowing me to see another day. For You are a mighty, awesome, magnificent, and amazing God. I thank You for Your mercy, grace, and favor. I take my time to praise You and to worship You for being my healer (Jehovah Rapha), deliverer (Jehovah Mephalti), and my rock in whom I take refuge.

### CONFESSION

Heavenly Father, You said in Your Word, according to 1 John 1:9, if we confess our sins, You are faithful and just to forgive us our sins and to cleanse us from all unrighteousness. God, I'm sorry for falling short in _____ and that my actions in _____ haven't lived up to Your expectations. I repent for not doing_____ when I should have done_____

. Heavenly Father, I let go of all offense, bitterness, anger, and disappointment, and I release it all unto You. I forgive _____, who have hurt me, disappointed me, and caused me any harm. You said in Your Word to forgive other people when they sin against me so that You, heavenly Father, will also forgive me (Matthew 6:14). I receive Your forgiveness. I have no condemnation in Christ (Romans 8:1), and I thank You for helping me to do better the next time. In Jesus's name. Amen.

## THANKSGIVING

I thank You, Lord, for Your unconditional love toward me. I thank You, heavenly Father, for being Jehovah Keren-Yish'I, the horn of my salvation. I thank You, Lord, for being my rock, my fortress, and my savior. My God is my rock, in whom I find protection. He is my shield, the power that saves me, and my place of safety and my stronghold (Psalm 18:2). I thank You for being my refuge and strength, a very present help in my time of trouble (Psalm 46:1). I bless Your holy name, and I am thankful that Your holy Word is forever true.

## SUPPLICATION

## DELIVERANCE

Father, in the name of Jesus, I lift up to You Your people today and everyone who is going through a challenging time in this world.

I also bring before You my children and grandchildren, family, spouse, friends, coworkers, supervisors, governmental leaders, and the body of Christ. I ask in the name of Jesus for You to comfort them with Your Holy Spirit and give them Your peace that surpasses all understanding, which guards their hearts and minds in Christ Jesus (Philippians 4:7). I also ask that You grant them Your mercy, grace, and favor as they go through their day and deal with every circumstance that they must face. Your Word says many are the afflictions of the righteous, but You, Jehovah Mephalti, will deliver them out of them all (Psalm 34:19).

For You are our deliverer, and You will never put more on Your people than they can bear (1 Corinthians 10:13). You said in Your Word that You will never leave us or forsake us (Hebrews 13:5). For You never leave the righteous forsaken nor His descendants begging for bread (Psalm 37:25).

You said in Your Word that when the enemy comes in like a flood, the Spirit of the Lord will lift up a standard, our Lord and Savior Jesus Christ, against him (Isaiah 59:19). Therefore, I declare in the name of Jesus that You came to give them life and life more abundantly (John 10:10). They shall see the goodness of the Lord in the land of the living (Psalm 27:13)! With long life, You shall satisfy them and show them Your salvation, which is deliverance, health, safety, and victory (Psalm 91:16).

Heavenly Father, I thank You for being their deliverer. I declare in the name of Jesus that they will put on the full armor of God so that when the day of evil comes, they may be able to stand their ground and, after they have done everything, to stand (Ephesians 6:13)! I pray that they will trust and believe the truth concerning the Word of God over any person and during any challenging times throughout their lives or any circumstance (1 Peter 5:9). Father, in the name of Jesus, I pray that as they submit themselves unto God and resist the devil, he (the devil) will flee from them (James 4:7).

I pray in the name of Jesus that the Lord bless them and keep them; may He make His face shine upon them and be gracious to them; may the Lord lift up His countenance upon them and give them peace (Numbers 6:23–26).


## FAVOR

I declare in the name of Jesus that I belong to the generation of the upright and that I am blessed (Psalm 112:2).

I declare in the name of Jesus that I am blessed and highly favored because I will never let Your loving devotion and faithfulness leave me; I bind them around my neck, and I write them on the tablet on my heart (Proverbs 3:4).

I declare in the name of Jesus that I have favor in the sight of God and with humanity. As I trust in the Lord with all my heart, lean not to my own understanding, and acknowledge Him in all my ways, I am confident that You, God Almighty, will continue to direct my paths (Proverbs 3:5–6).

I declare in the name of Jesus that this is my set time of favor (Psalm 102:13).

I declare in the name of Jesus that I have the favor of the Lord that lasts for a lifetime, and it confirms the works of my hands (Psalms 30:5, 90:17).

I declare in the name of Jesus that You are causing everything to work together for my good because I love You and I am called according to Your purpose (Romans 8:28).

I declare in the name of Jesus that You are causing Your grace to abound toward me so that I will always have all sufficiency in all things and I will have abundance for every good work (2 Corinthians 9:8).

I declare in the name of Jesus that my gifts are making room for me, and they are bringing me before great and mighty people (Proverbs 18:16).

I declare in the name of Jesus that You are opening doors for me that no person can shut (Revelation 3:8). For my trust, confidence, and faith are in You, God Almighty.

## Loosing Forth the Word of God

Your Word says that this is the victory that conquers the world, which is our faith (1 John 5:4)! You said in Your Word that if I have faith the size of a mustard seed and say to this mountain to be thou removed and cast into the sea, that it shall be done (Matthew 17:20). Therefore, I speak to every mountain of doubt, fear, unbelief, debt, and lack, and I cast it into the sea in the name of Jesus.

I declare in the name of Jesus that I have clarity and a sound mind. Your Word tells me that the memory of the righteous is blessed (Proverbs 10:7). Therefore, as I put my hope, trust, and confidence in You, heavenly Father, I can never be disappointed (Romans 10:11).

I declare in the name of Jesus that You are my refuge and strength, my very present help in the time of trouble, and therefore I will not fear. I will not be afraid of the terror by night or of the destruction that lays waste at noon. For a thousand will fall at my side and ten thousand at my right hand, but it (the danger, or whatever *it* may be) shall not come near me (Psalm 46:1–2; Psalm 91:5–7). I declare in the name of Jesus that You did not give me the spirit of fear but of power, love, and a sound mind (2 Timothy 1:7).

I declare in the name of Jesus that evil tidings shall not come near my children, family, home, and the neighborhood or city in which I live. I stand firm in my faith in Jesus Christ, and I push back the spirit of darkness over the region that you have given me jurisdiction over, and I decree and declare Your Holy Word, that the gates of hell shall not prevail against us and that the weapons of my warfare are not carnal but are mighty through God to the pulling down of strongholds (2 Corinthians 10:4; Matthew 16:18).

For You have given me the keys of the kingdom to bind and to loose according to Matthew 18:18. Therefore, I decree and declare in the name of Jesus that whatever I bind on earth will be bound in heaven, and whatever I loose on earth will be loosed in heaven.

I bind up the spirits of pride, strife, discord, hate, jealousy, racism, retaliation, false religion, lawlessness, rebellion, falling away from the faith, fear, anxiety, mental illnesses, infirmities, sorcery, witchcraft, hexes, spells, and voodoo; the accuser of the brethren; the spirit of Jezebel; the spirit of Korah; and the spirit of Absalom in the name of Jesus, and I loose forth the Word of God!

In the name of Jesus Christ of Nazareth, I loose forth and declare 1 Peter 4:8, that the love of God covers a multitude of sins.

I loose forth 1 Corinthians 16:13, and I declare in the name of Jesus that I will be on alert, I will stand firm in the faith, and I will be strong and courageous in everything that I do.

I loose forth Philippians 4:6–7, and I declare in the name of Jesus that I will be anxious for nothing, but in everything by prayer and supplication, I will make my requests known to God.

I loose forth 1 Peter 5:7, and I declare in the name of Jesus that I will cast my cares upon You because You care for me, and I know that You will sustain me.

I loose forth Philippians 2:4, and I declare in the name of Jesus that I will not look out for my own interest but for the interest of others.

I loose forth John 8:32, and I declare in the name of Jesus that my unsaved loved ones, this world, and my country will know the truth, and the truth shall set them free—that Jesus Christ is Lord and that there are no other gods beside Him.

I loose forth Psalm 107:20, and I declare in the name of Jesus that You, Jehovah Rapha, sent Your Word to heal me and to deliver me from all destruction.

I loose forth Isaiah 53:5, and I declare that Jesus Christ of Nazareth was wounded for my transgressions, bruised for my iniquities, and the chastisement for my peace was upon Him, and by His stripes I was healed. Jehovah Rapha, I receive Your Word concerning my healing, and I walk in it in the name of Jesus.

I declare in the name of Jesus that healing is the children's bread and that I am your child (Mark 7:27).

I loose forth Revelations 12:11 and declare in the name of Jesus that I overcome by the blood of the Lamb and by the word of my testimony.

I loose forth Numbers 23:8, and I declare in the name of Jesus that no man can curse whom God has blessed.

I loose forth Ephesians 2:6 in the name of Jesus, that God raised me up with Christ and seated me with Him in the heavenly realms in Christ Jesus.

I declare in the name of Jesus that I shall be relentless to my call to prayer, intercession, decrees, declaration, praise, worship, and in all things I was created to do here on this earth, regardless of my circumstances.

I declare in the name of Jesus that although I may be hard-pressed on every side, I am not crushed, perplexed, in despair, persecuted, abandoned, struck down, or destroyed (2 Corinthians 4:8–9).

I declare in the name of Jesus that the same power that raised Jesus Christ from the dead is in me. It is He who raised Christ Jesus from the dead who will also give me life to my mortal body through His Spirit who dwells in me (Romans 8:11)!

I declare in the name of Jesus that I am more than a conqueror through Him who loved me. For I am convinced that neither death nor life, nor angels, nor principalities, nor things present, nor things to come, nor powers, nor height, nor depth, nor any other created thing will be able to separate me from the love of God, which is in Christ Jesus our Lord (Romans 8:38–39).

I decree and declare by faith in Almighty God that the wicked will be shaken and that wickedness will not prevail in our nation, in its laws, decrees, or leaders, in our homes, our dwelling places, our children, grandchildren, and great-grandchildren, in ministries, businesses, economic systems, government systems, judicial systems, educational systems, and financial systems and institutions, in the name of Jesus. Therefore, I decree and declare in the name of Jesus that the powers of darkness are pushed back because of the infallible, prevailing, and everlasting Word of God.

For the Word of God is alive and active, sharper than any double-edged sword; it penetrates even to dividing soul and spirit, joints and marrow; it judges the thoughts and attitudes of the heart (Hebrews 4:12).

Your Word, heavenly Father, is truth and is the final authority in all of the affairs of life (John 17:17)!

Your Word, heavenly Father, does not return to You void, and it shall not return unto You void. Instead, it shall accomplish that which You please, and it shall prosper in the thing whereto you sent it. You hasten to Your Word to perform it. For our God is not a man, that he should lie, neither the son of man, that he should repent (Isaiah 55:11; Jeremiah 1:12; Numbers 23:19).

I thank You, God, for hearing me and answering my prayers. For the eyes of the Lord are over the righteous, and his ears are inclined to their prayers (1 Peter 3:12; Psalm 34:15). You said in Your Word, according to Isaiah 65:24 (Good News Translation), "Even before they finish praying to me, I will answer their prayers." For You are not slow concerning Your promises. For all the promises of God in Him are yes, and in Him amen, to the glory of God through us (1 John 5:15; 2 Peter 3:9; 2 Corinthians 1:20). For this, I worship You, and I give You all glory, all honor, and all praise, being the only true and Living God! In Jesus's mighty name. Amen.

# Personalize Your
## Prayers, Decrees & Declarations

# 2

## PRAYER AND DECLARATIONS FOR OUR CHILDREN

### ADORATION

Bless the Lord, O my soul, and all that is within me. Bless His holy name. Bless the Lord, O my soul, and forget none of His benefits, who pardons all your iniquities, who heals all your diseases, who redeems your life from the pit, who crowns you with loving-kindness and compassion, who satisfies your years with good things so that your youth is renewed like the eagle (Psalm 103:1–5).

### CONFESSION

Heavenly Father, You said in Your Word, according to 1 John 1:9, if we confess our sins, You are faithful and just to forgive us our sins and to cleanse us from all unrighteousness. God, I'm sorry for falling short in _____ and that my actions in _____ haven't lived up to Your expectations. I repent for not doing_____ when I should have done_____. Heavenly Father, I let go of all offense, bitterness, anger, and disappointment, and I release it all unto You. I forgive _____, who have hurt me, disappointed me, and caused me any harm. You said in Your Word to forgive other people when they sin against me so that You, heavenly Father, will also forgive me (Matthew 6:14). I receive Your forgiveness. I have no condemnation in Christ (Romans 8:1), and I thank You for helping me to do better the next time. In Jesus's name. Amen.

## Thanksgiving

Oh give thanks unto the Lord. Call upon His name. Make known His deeds among the peoples. Sing to Him. Sing praises to Him. Speak to all His wonders. Glory in His holy name. Let the heart of those who seek the Lord be glad. Seek the Lord and His strength. Seek His face continually (1 Chronicles 16:8–11).

## Supplication

### Children

Father, in the name of Jesus, I thank You for my children.

I declare in the name of Jesus that Your plans for my children are good, plans not to harm them but to prosper them and to give them a future and a hope (Jeremiah 29:11).

I declare in the name of Jesus that You formed my children in the womb and that You knew them before they were born. You set them apart and appointed them as prophets to the nations (Jeremiah 1:5).

For You said in Your Word that in these last days, You will pour out Your spirit upon all people and that our sons and daughters will prophesy, our young men will see visions, our old men will dream dreams (Joel 2:28; Acts 2:17).

I call those things that are not as though they were concerning my children (Romans 4:17).

I declare in the name of Jesus that my children are coming out of darkness and into your marvelous light, that they are no longer lost but found, and that they are saved and filled with your Holy Spirit and fire (1Peter 2:9).

I plead the blood of Jesus over my children.

I bind and rebuke every plot, scheme, and trap of the enemy that is coming against my children.

I bind up the spirits of confusion, lawlessness, rebellion, and the antichrist, in the name of Jesus. I cover my children with the Word of God, the love of God, and the blood of Jesus Christ of Nazareth.

I declare in the name of Jesus that my children are being set free and protected by the Word of God.

For the Word of God is quick, powerful, and sharper than any two-edged sword, piercing even to the dividing asunder of soul and spirit, and of the joints and marrow, and is a discerner of the thoughts and intents of the heart (Hebrews 4:12).

I declare in the name of Jesus that the Love of God covers a multitude of sins, and Your love for my children, Father God, never fails (1 Peter 4:8; 1 Corinthians 13:8).

I declare in the name of Jesus that the blood of Jesus cleanses my children from all sin, and their hearts are sprinkled and purified by the blood of Jesus from an evil conscience (Hebrews 10:22; 1 John 1:7).

I thank You for healing my children from any and all behavioral, mental, and physical challenges. I declare in the name of Jesus that by the stripes of Jesus, my children were healed (1 Peter 2:24). I thank You, Jesus, that You took up my children's infirmities and bore their diseases (Matthew 8:17). For You are the balm of Gilead (Jeremiah 8:21–22). For You are Jehovah Rapha, the Lord who heals, and there is nothing impossible for you to do (Exodus 15:26; Luke 1:37).

I take You at Your word concerning my children and their future.

I declare in the name of Jesus that my children shall have the best education, attend the best colleges and universities, and obtain the best jobs and careers. They shall be equally yoked in their marriages, and their future children shall rise up and call them blessed (2 Corinthians 6:14; Proverbs 31:28).

I decree and declare in the name of Jesus that my children will feed off of the wealth of the nations, and in their riches they shall boast (Isaiah 61:6).

I decree and declare in the name of Jesus that all of my children shall be taught of the Lord, and great shall be the peace of my children (Isaiah 54:13).

I decree and declare in the name of Jesus that my children have the mind of Christ and that they know the voice of the Lord. For Your Word says that "my sheep shall know my voice and the voice of another, they shall not follow" (1 Corinthians 2:16; John 10:27).

I decree and declare in the name of Jesus that because the Word of God is in my children's heart, they will not sin against You (Psalm 119:11).

I decree and declare in the name of Jesus that my children are blessed and that they do not walk in the counsel of the ungodly, nor stand in the path of sinners, nor sit in the seat of the scornful, but their delight is in the law of the Lord, and in His law they meditate day and night. I decree and declare in the name of Jesus that my children shall be like a tree planted by the rivers of water that brings forth its fruit in its season, whose leaf also shall not wither, and whatever they do, they shall prosper (Psalm 1:1–3).

I decree and declare in the name of Jesus that my children shall see the goodness of the Lord in the land of the living and that You came to give them life—and life more abundantly. I decree and declare in the name of Jesus, with long life, You shall satisfy them, and that above all things, they shall prosper and be in good health as their souls prosper. (Psalm 27:13; John 10:10; 3 John 1:2).

I thank You, heavenly Father, that You will make all grace abound toward my children with all sufficiency, so that they will have abundance for every good work (2 Corinthians 9:8).

Thank You, heavenly Father, for fulfilling every promise and prophecy You have ordained in Your Word concerning my children. In Jesus's name. Amen.

# Personalize Your
## Prayers, Decrees & Declarations

## DAY

# 3

## GREATER WORKS

## BEING AN OVERCOMER

### ADORATION

But You, O Lord, are a shield about me, my glory and the one who lifts my head. I was crying to the Lord with my voice, and He answered me from His holy mountain. I lay down and slept; I awoke, for the Lord sustained me (Psalm 3:3–5). For You are my keeper and my protector, and I bless Your holy name.

### CONFESSION

Heavenly Father, You said in Your Word, according to 1 John 1:9, if we confess our sins, You are faithful and just to forgive us our sins and to cleanse us from all unrighteousness. God, I'm sorry for falling short in _____ and that my actions in _____ haven't lived up to Your expectations. I repent for not doing_____ when I should have done_____ . Heavenly Father, I let go of all offense, bitterness, anger, and disappointment, and I release it all unto You. I forgive _____, who have hurt me, disappointed me, and caused me any harm. You said in Your Word to forgive other people when they sin against me so that You, heavenly Father, will also forgive me (Matthew 6:14). I receive Your forgiveness. I have no

condemnation in Christ (Romans 8:1), and I thank You for helping me to do better the next time. In Jesus's name. Amen.

## THANKSGIVING

I will give thanks to the Lord with all my heart. I will tell of Your wonders. I will be glad and exult in You. I will sing praises to Your name, O Most High (Psalm 9:1–2).

## SUPPLICATION

## GREATER WORKS

Father, in the name of Jesus, I thank You for Your mighty works and the greater works that I shall do.

You said in Your Word greater works that I shall do, because you have gone to the Father (John 14:12).

I declare in the name of Jesus the spirit of the Lord is upon me, because You have anointed me to bring good news to the afflicted, to bind up the brokenhearted, to proclaim liberty to the captives and freedom to the prisoners, to proclaim the favorable year of the Lord and the vengeance of our God (Isaiah 61:1–2).

I thank You, Lord, for equipping me and making room for me, because You are Jehovah Rehoboth (Genesis 26:22).

I thank You, Lord, for strengthening me with Your Word, Holy Spirit, Your power, and Your anointing to be a blessing to all people—financially, physically, spiritually and emotionally.

## BEING AN OVERCOMER

I declare in the name of Jesus that I shall overcome opposition and every plan, plot, and scheme of the enemy. For You have given me power to tread on serpents and scorpions and over all of the power of the enemy, and nothing shall by any means harm me (Luke 10:19).

I command the powers of darkness and evil to flee from me in the name of Jesus. I put a demand on Your Word, and I command my healing and my deliverance in the name of Jesus.

For You sent Your Word to heal me and to deliver me from all destruction (Psalm 107:20).

Hallelujah! I declare in the name of Jesus that as I bless my enemies and love my enemies, You, almighty, omnipotent, and sovereign God, will cause my enemies to be for me and for You, the King of kings and Lord of lords, in the name of Jesus.

I thank You, Father, for preparing a table before me in the presence of my enemies (Psalm 23:5).

I declare in the name of Jesus that with Your presence, power, peace, and Holy Spirit, I will love my enemies and pray for those who persecute me (Matthew 5:44).

I declare in the name of Jesus that if my enemies are hungry, I will feed them, and I will give them water when they are thirsty (Romans 12:20).

I declare, in the name of Jesus, that I will not return evil for evil, and instead, I will depart from evil and do good, and I will seek peace and pursue it (Psalm 34:14).

I declare in the name of Jesus that I am strong in You and in the power of Your might (Ephesians 6:10).

I declare in the name of Jesus that I can do all things through Jesus Christ that strengthen me (Philippians 4:13).

I declare in the name of Jesus that I can write books, start a business, go to school, finish school, obtain a degree, obtain a certification, pass the test, pass the interviews, receive job offers with excellent benefits and pay, get the promotion, and give the promotion in the name of Jesus.

For I am more than a conqueror through Jesus Christ, who loves me (Romans 8:37)!

I declare in the name of Jesus that with You, all things are possible (Matthew 19:26).

You are a great and awesome God! All praise, glory, and honor belong to You. I thank You for hearing me each and every time I pray, and I thank You for answering my prayers, in Jesus's name. Amen (1 John 5:15).

# Personalize Your
## Prayers, Decrees & Declarations

## CHURCH LEADERS
## HEALING FOR CHURCH LEADERS
## HEALING FOR OUR NATION

### ADORATION

O Lord, our Lord, how majestic is Your name in all the earth, who have displayed Your splendor above the heavens! From the mouth of infants and nursing babes, You have established strength (Psalm 8:1–2).

### CONFESSION

Heavenly Father, You said in Your Word, according to 1 John 1:9, if we confess our sins, You are faithful and just to forgive us our sins and to cleanse us from all unrighteousness. God, I'm sorry for falling short in _____ and that my actions in _____ haven't lived up to Your expectations. I repent for not doing_____ when I should have done_____ . Heavenly Father, I let go of all offense, bitterness, anger, and disappointment, and I release it all unto You. I forgive _____, who have hurt me, disappointed me, and caused me any harm. You said in Your Word to forgive other people when they sin against me so that You, heavenly Father, will also forgive me (Matthew 6:14). I receive Your forgiveness. I have no

condemnation in Christ (Romans 8:1), and I thank You for helping me to do better the next time. In Jesus's name. Amen.

## THANKSGIVING

I thank You for Your Word. The words of the Lord are pure words, as silver tried in a furnace on the earth, refined seven times (Psalm 12:6). I thank You that Your Word remains forever. The grass withers, and the flowers fade, but the Word of our God stands forever (Isaiah 40:8).

## SUPPLICATION

## CHURCH LEADERS

Father, in the name of Jesus, I lift up to You our church leaders—those within the fivefold ministry (apostles, prophets, evangelists, pastors, and teachers) and those who serve as leaders within the ministry of helps.

I declare in the name of Jesus a hedge of protection around them and a hedge of protection around their marriages, families, children, employment, ministry, business, life, health, strength, finances, and every asset that they possess.

I thank You, Father, for protecting them from danger seen and unseen, evil seen and unseen, and from every snare, trap, trick, or scheme of the devil and his imps, in the name of Jesus.

I declare in the name of Jesus Your Word according to Psalm 91:10–11, that no evil shall befall them, nor will any plague come near their dwelling places, and that Your angels are taking charge concerning them and guarding them in all of their ways.

I declare in the name of Jesus that as they delight themselves in You, You will give them the desires of their heart (Psalm 37:4).

I speak strength to their physical bodies and declare Your Word according to Deuteronomy 33:25; as their day goes, so shall their strength be.

I declare in the name of Jesus Ephesians 6:10, that they are strong in You and in the power of Your might.

I declare in the name of Jesus Nehemiah 8:10, that the joy of the Lord is their strength.

I declare in the name of Jesus Acts 17:28; it is in You that they live, move, and have their being.

I come against every distraction and hindrance from the enemy, and I declare in the name of Jesus that the Word of God will dwell richly in our church leaders, with all wisdom, teaching, and admonishing one another with psalms and hymns and spiritual songs, singing with thankfulness in their hearts to God, and whatever they do in word or deed, they will do it in the name of the Lord Jesus, giving thanks through Him to God the Father (Colossians 3:16–17). I pray that they will not be deceived, tricked, enticed, or tempted by the devil, in Jesus's name.

I declare in the name of Jesus that as they humble themselves before the Lord and resist the devil, the devil must flee from them (James 4:7)!

## Healing for Church Leaders

I declare divine healing for our church leaders, in the name of Jesus.

Spirit of infirmity (name the infirmity), I speak to you, and I command you to bow down and flee from our church leaders in the name of Jesus! I resist (name the infirmity), and I command it to go back to pits of hell where it came from and to never return again, in the name of Jesus!

I declare Philippians 2:10, that at the name of Jesus, every knee shall bow, of things in heaven, and things in earth, and things under the earth. I declare Jesus is Lord over their physical bodies and mental faculties. I declare in the name of Jesus that their bodies are the temple of the Holy Spirit (1 Corinthians 6:19).

I declare in the name of Jesus that our church leaders have the minds of Christ and that their thinking and thought patterns are clear and in alignment with the plans and purpose of Christ, to bring glory to God in everything they say and do, to restore humanity to Christ, and to be powerful witnesses to the lost, so that salvation can manifest throughout the earth.

In the name of Jesus, I cast down imaginations and every high thing that exalteth itself against the knowledge of God, and I bring into captivity every thought to the obedience of Christ (1 Corinthians 10:5).

I declare in the name of Jesus that our church leaders have been cleansed by the blood of Jesus Christ, who is our healer and high priest who forever lives to make intercession for them (Hebrews 7:25).

I declare in the name of Jesus that sickness and disease cannot stay in their bodies! For our Lord and Savior, Jesus Christ, was wounded for their transgressions, bruised for their iniquities and the chastisement of their peace was upon Him, and by the stripes of Jesus, our church leaders are healed (Isaiah 53:5).

I thank You, Jesus, that You came to give our church leaders life—and life more abundantly (John 10:10)—and that You are the Good Shepherd, the one who laid down His life for His sheep (John 10:11).

Therefore, I speak life to our church leaders. I declare in the name of Jesus that with long life, You shall satisfy them and show them Your salvation (Psalm 91:16). They shall not die but live and declare the works of the Lord (Psalm 118:17)! I pray that in all respects, they may prosper and be in good health, just as their souls prosper (3 John 1:2).

Jehovah Rapha, I thank You for being their healer, and I thank you that You sent Your Word to heal them and to deliver them from their destruction (Psalm 107:20). I declare that by the stripes of Jesus, they are healed (Isaiah 53:5). Your Word says that many are the afflictions of the righteous, but the Lord delivers them out of them all (Psalm 39:14).

I thank You, Jehovah Nissi, for being our banner (Exodus 17:15)! I thank You, Jesus, for being the ultimate sacrifice on the cross, for being the bread of life and the Living Word of God—life to those who find them and health to one's whole body (Matthew 6:11; Hebrew 4:12; Proverbs 4:22).

Thank You, Jehovah Nissi, for being a banner and protector for our church leaders. I declare Isaiah 59:19, so shall they fear the name of the Lord from the west and His glory from the rising of the sun. When the enemy shall come in like a flood, the Spirit of the Lord shall lift up a standard against him. I declare in the name of Jesus that no weapon formed against our church leaders shall prosper, and every tongue that rises against them in judgment, You shall condemn (Isaiah 54:17).

## HEALING FOR OUR NATION

Father, in the name of Jesus, I lift up to You our nation. I have total faith and confidence in You. You said in Your Word, according to Luke 1:37, for with God nothing, shall be impossible. Therefore, I trust You to heal and restore our nation to be a place of no incurable disease(s) (name the disease/s). I declare in the name of Jesus a healthy, safe, and thriving nation with an abundance of wealth and resources—a land flowing with milk and honey, according to Exodus 3:8.

I declare Your Word according to 2 Chronicles 7:14, in the name of Jesus, that says, "If my people, who are called by my name, will humble themselves and pray and seek my face and turn from their wicked ways, then I will hear from heaven, and I will forgive their sin and will heal their land."

Father, in the name of Jesus, I repent of my sins and for the sins of this nation, and I seek Your face. Forgive our nation for falling short and for violating Your holy Word. Forgive us for engaging in lawlessness, immorality, rebellion, and disobedience that has caused chaos and mass destruction to our land.

I pray Your Word according to Hebrews 3:12–13, that our nation will take care, and as brethren, that there will not be in any of us an evil, unbelieving heart that falls away from the Living God. I pray in the name of Jesus that as a nation, we will encourage one another day after day, as long as it is still called today, and that none of us will be hardened by the deceitfulness of sin.

I pray in the name of Jesus, that today, if the people of our nation hear Your voice, they will not harden their hearts (Hebrews 3:15). Father, in the name of Jesus, I ask that You give the people of our nation a new heart and put a new spirit in them; remove from them their hearts of stone and give them hearts of flesh (Ezekiel 36:26). Father, in the name of Jesus, I pray for repentance, revival, and salvation for our nation.

I declare in the name of Jesus a nation that seeks Your face and that has turned their hearts back to God.

I thank You, God, for hearing my prayers and for answering me in my time of need. I thank You, heavenly Father, for protecting and healing our church leaders and for healing our nation. So be it unto us according to Your Word. In the name of Jesus. Amen.

# Personalize Your
## Prayers, Decrees & Declarations

# 5

## SALVATION

### ADORATION

Father, in the name of Jesus, I thank You for the ultimate sacrifice You made for us on the cross. I thank You, Jesus, for shedding Your blood on Calvary for us. I honor You, exalt You, appreciate You, and love You for Your faithfulness, Your loving-kindness, Your mercy, and Your grace.

You keep on sustaining me during this hour (Psalm 3:5). You continue to show Yourself strong through me (Psalm 18:32; 68:28). You continue to fight my battles (Exodus 14:14; Deuteronomy 3:22). You continue to bless me and make my name great (Genesis 12:2). You continue to feed me, clothe me, provide for me, and keep me in my right mind (Genesis 22:14; Luke 8:35; 2 Corinthians 5:13). You supply all of my needs according to Your riches in glory in Christ Jesus (Philippians 4:19).

You continue to break through, break out, and break forth for me (2 Samuel 5:20; 1 Chronicles 14:11). For You are Jehovah Rehoboth, my God who makes room for me (Genesis 26:22). You cause my gift to make room for me and bring me before great men (Proverbs 18:16). For You are sovereign, and You are holy (Acts 4:24; Revelation 4:8). You are worthy to be praised (Psalm 145:3)! There is no other God beside You, and there is no other God like my God. I worship You because You are Jehovah Mephalti, my deliverer, and You are Jehovah Keren-Yish'I, the horn of my salvation.

## CONFESSION

Heavenly Father, You said in Your Word, according to 1 John 1:9, if we confess our sins, You are faithful and just to forgive us our sins and to cleanse us from all unrighteousness. God, I'm sorry for falling short in _____ and that my actions in _____ haven't lived up to Your expectations. I repent for not doing_____ when I should have done_____ . Heavenly Father, I let go of all offense, bitterness, anger, and disappointment, and I release it all unto You. I forgive _____, who have hurt me, disappointed me, and caused me any harm. You said in Your Word to forgive other people when they sin against me so that You, heavenly Father, will also forgive me (Matthew 6:14). I receive Your forgiveness. I have no condemnation in Christ (Romans 8:1), and I thank You for helping me to do better the next time. In Jesus's name. Amen.

## THANKSGIVING

I thank You, Lord, for Your faithfulness. You are the everlasting God, the Lord, the creator of the ends of the earth. I thank You that You never become weary or tired. Your understanding is inscrutable. I thank You for being a compassionate God. You give strength to the weary and increase the power of the weak (Isaiah 40:28–29).

## SUPPLICATION

### DECLARATIONS FOR SALVATION

As I go forth in my calling and in the anointing of God and in the power and authority of the Holy Spirit, I declare in the name of Jesus that I will continue to exercise and put to practice Jude 1:20– 23, which says, "But you beloved, building yourselves up on your most holy faith, praying in the Holy Spirit, keep yourselves in the love of God, waiting anxiously for the mercy of our Lord Jesus Christ to eternal life. And have mercy on some who are doubting, save others, and snatch them out of the fire."

Father, in the name of Jesus, I bring before you my unsaved loved ones and those on this earth who are lost, not saved, and living in sin, engaging in lawlessness, rebellion, and sexual immorality.

Father, in the name of Jesus Christ of Nazareth, I plead the blood of Jesus Christ over them. I call their names out (name them) continuously before you, and I declare the Word of God over them, according to Ezekiel 36:26, that you will give them a new heart and put a new spirit within them and that you will take the heart of stone out of them and give them a heart of flesh.

I bind up any and all matters of confusion within their mind, and I loose forth clarity within their mind in the name of Jesus. I declare total healing of past hurts, trauma, exploitation, abuse, and neglect, in the name of Jesus. I declare in the name of Jesus total deliverance of any involvement of drug and alcohol addiction, occults, curses, bewitchment, and false religion, in the name of Jesus.

I declare in the name of Jesus that You, heavenly Father, are continually sending forth divine labors across their path and that You are continually setting up divine appointments for the Gospel of Jesus Christ to be ministered to them. I pray in the name of Jesus that those who are not saved and who are lost will accept Jesus Christ as their Lord and Savior.

For You are the Alpha and the Omega, the one who is and who was and who is to come, the Almighty (Revelation 1:8)!

I decree and declare in the name of Jesus, according to Luke 19:9–10, that today salvation has come to their house. For the Son of Man came to seek and to save the lost!

I decree and declare Your Word, Jehovah Keren-Yish'I, Acts 16:31, that they will believe in the Lord Jesus, and they will be saved, both them and their household.

I declare in the name of Jesus Ephesians 2:4, that they will come to an understanding and realization that because of Your great love toward us, God, who is rich in mercy, made us alive with Christ even when we were dead in transgressions and that it is by grace we have been saved!

For You are not slow in keeping your promise, as some understand slowness. Instead, You are patient with us, not wanting anyone to perish but that everyone shall come to repentance, according to 2 Peter 3:9.

Father, You said in Your Word that if they confess their sins, You are faithful and just to forgive them of their sins and to cleanse them from all unrighteousness (1 John 1:9).

For You said in Your Word in Acts 2:21, "And it shall be that everyone who calls on the name of the Lord will be saved."

I pray in the name of Jesus that they will confess with their mouths that Jesus is Lord and believe in their hearts that God raised Him from the dead, and they will be saved (Romans 10:9). You said in Your Word, according to Romans 10:13, that whoever will call on the name of the Lord will be saved, and according to Acts 16:3, if they believe in the Lord Jesus, they will be saved, as well as their household.

I pray in the name of Jesus that those who are not saved shall repent, each and every one of them, and be baptized in the name of Jesus Christ for the forgiveness of their sins, that they will receive the gift of the Holy Spirit, and that they will continue to devote themselves to the apostles' teaching and to fellowship, to the breaking of bread, and to prayer! So be it, according to Your Word in Acts 2:38 and verse 42.

Therefore, I decree and declare in the name of Jesus that the Lord will continue to add to our numbers daily those who are being saved (Acts 2:47).

I declare in accordance with Acts 6:3, 5, and 8, in the name of Jesus, that I will be continually filled with the Spirit and wisdom. I will be continually full of faith, full of Your Holy Spirit, full of grace, and full of power to teach and preach the Gospel of Jesus Christ, to totally heal, deliver, and set free all those who are sick, bound, oppressed, depressed, and afflicted with unclean spirits, in the name of Jesus.

I declare in the name of Jesus that I will not be deceived by the works, snares, traps, false signs, false wonders, false words, and works of the devil.

I decree and declare in the name of Jesus 1 Peter 5:8–9. I will be sober, vigilant, and alert, because I understand that my enemy, the devil, prowls around like a roaring lion, seeking someone to devour. I declare in the name of Jesus that I will resist him and stand firm in the faith, because I know that the family of believers throughout the world is undergoing the same kind of sufferings.

I declare in the name of Jesus that after I have suffered for a little while, the God of all grace, who called me to His eternal glory in Christ, will Himself perfect, confirm, strengthen, and establish me (1 Peter 5:10).

You are a great and mighty God, and I bless Your great and mighty name! Thank You, Father God, for giving us Your only begotten Son, Jesus Christ, to die on the cross for our sins. Thank You, Jesus, for salvation. Thank You, Father God, for hastening to Your Word to perform it as a result of this decree, declaration, and prayer. In Jesus's name. Amen.

# Personalize Your
## Prayers, Decrees & Declarations

<br/>

———— DAY ————

# 6

## PERSONAL SUPPLICATION
## PROTECTION OF LOVED ONES
## SPIRITUAL WARFARE

### ADORATION

Shout joyfully to God, all the earth. Sing the glory of his name. Make His name glorious. Say to God, "How awesome are Your works! Because of the greatness of Your power, Your enemies will cringe before You. All the earth will worship You and will sing praises to You. They will sing praises to Your name" (Psalm 66:1–4). For You are the great Jehovah! You are Jehovah Shalom, our peace, and Jehovah Nissi, our banner! Bless Your holy name!

### CONFESSION

Heavenly Father, You said in Your Word, according to 1 John 1:9, if we confess our sins, You are faithful and just to forgive us our sins and to cleanse us from all unrighteousness. God, I'm sorry for falling short in _____ and that my actions in _____ haven't lived up to Your expectations. I repent for not doing_____ when I should have done_____ . Heavenly Father, I let go of all offense, bitterness, anger, and disappointment, and I release it all unto You. I forgive _____, who have hurt

me, disappointed me, and caused me any harm. You said in Your Word to forgive other people when they sin against me so that You, heavenly Father, will also forgive me (Matthew 6:14). I receive Your forgiveness. I have no condemnation in Christ (Romans 8:1), and I thank You for helping me to do better the next time. In Jesus's name. Amen.


## THANKSGIVING

Father, in the name of Jesus, I thank You for Your mercy and grace. I thank You for Your loving-kindness that You continue to display toward me. Day after day, You fill me with Your spirit. You strengthen me, renew my mind, and continue to cause me to advance the kingdom of God for Your glory. I thank You for Your sovereignty. For You are Lord, and You will reign forever and ever (Exodus 15:8). For Your kingdom will be an everlasting kingdom, and all rulers will worship and obey You (Daniel 7:7).

You alone are the Most High over all the earth (Psalm 83:18). For your dominion is an everlasting dominion that will not pass away, and Your kingdom is one that will never be destroyed (Daniel 7:14).

I worship You because You are my God, and You are my Father. You are the great Jehovah, the everlasting God, King of kings, and Lord of lords! You are Alpha and Omega, and I thank You for Your ultimate sacrifice, Jesus Christ, who died on the cross for my sins. I magnify Your name, Jesus. For You are Christ, the holy and anointed one, the Prince of Peace, the root and offspring of David, the morning star, the bread of life, and the Living Word of God!

I thank You, heavenly Father, that You are moving Your hand on my behalf. I thank You, heavenly Father, that as I seek Your face through prayer and intercession, and as I boldly declare Your Word with the decrees and declarations You have placed on my heart, You are faithful and just to honor Your Word. You hasten to Your Word to perform it and You hear me each and every time that I pray (Jeremiah 1:12; 1 Peter 3:12; 1 John 5:15).

## Supplication

### Personal Supplication

For the eyes of the Lord are toward the righteous, and His ears attend to their prayers (1 Peter 3:12).

I declare Proverbs 28:1 in the name of Jesus, that I am righteous, and the righteous are as bold as a lion.

I declare in the name of Jesus that I am the righteousness of God in Christ Jesus and that as a righteous person in Christ Jesus, I shall inherit the land and dwell in it forever (2 Corinthians 5:21; Psalm 37:29).

According to Romans 8:11, I declare in the name of Jesus the same Spirit that raised Jesus Christ from the dead is within me.

I command my morning and speak to every situation concerning all of my affairs of life according to the Word of God, as is written in Hebrews 4:12, "For the Word of God is quick, and powerful, and sharper than any two edged sword, piercing even to the dividing asunder of soul and spirit, and of the joints and marrow, and is a discerner of the thoughts and intents of the heart."

I thank You, and I praise You for Your Word and that I have access to approach Your throne of grace with confidence, so that I may receive mercy and find grace to help me in my time of need (Hebrews 4:16).

I thank You, heavenly Father, that You said in your Word, according to 1 John 5:14, "This is the confidence that I have in You, whatever I ask according to Your will, You hear me, and that if I know that You hear me, then whatsoever I ask, I know that I have the petitions that I have asked of You."

### Protection of Loved Ones

Father, in the name of Jesus, I come before You with my petitions for my loved ones.

I declare that my loved ones who serve as earthly leaders and those who are unsaved will have a heart of repentance and will orchestrate and implement Godly legislation, policies, protocols, and procedures at the local, state, and federal levels. I pray in the name of Jesus that You, Father God, will relent, forgive us of our sins, and have mercy on our land.

I stand on Your Word concerning the healing for my loved ones.

Healing is the children's bread (Matthew 15:22–29).

I declare in the name of Jesus that it is Your will for my loved ones to be healed (Psalm 103:1–5)!

It is their right to walk in divine health and healing, and it is their covenant with You (Isaiah 53:5)!

I declare 1 Peter 2:24, that He himself bore our sins in his body on the cross, so that we might die to sin and live for righteousness, and by his wounds we have been healed.

I will continue to declare Psalm 91:10–11 over my loved ones, that no evil shall befall them, nor will any plague come near their dwelling place. For He will Give His angels charge concerning them and will guard them in all of their ways.

## Spiritual Warfare

I take dominion and authority, and I decree and declare Your written Word!

For You have given me the power to tread on serpents and scorpions and over all the power of the enemy, and nothing shall by any means hurt me (Luke 10:19).

I declare that the gates of hell shall not prevail against me in the name of Jesus (Matthew 16:18).

For this purpose, the Son of God was manifested, that He might destroy the works of the devil (1 John 3:8). Therefore, I declare that the works of the devil are destroyed over my home, family, marriage, relationships, city, region, finance, business, and ministry, in the name of Jesus!

I declare that the weapons of my warfare are not carnal but that they are mighty through God to the pulling down of strongholds, in the name of Jesus (2 Corinthians 10:7)!

You said in Your Word that I wrestle not against flesh and blood but against principalities, against powers, against the rulers of the darkness of this world, against spiritual wickedness in high places (Ephesians 6:12).

Therefore, I bind and rebuke every evil plan, plot, snare, and trap of the enemy, in the name of Jesus.

I disannul, dismantle, tear down, and utterly destroy every hindering spirit, every spirit of opposition, the accuser of the brothermen, every lie, every fault-finding spirit, criticism, satanic oppression, sickness, disease, poverty, lack, debt, and every demonic scheme that is trying to come against me concerning my home, family, marriage, relationships, city, region, finance, business, and ministry, in the name of Jesus!

Father, You said in Your Word that if You are for me, You are more than the whole world who is against me (Romans 8:31).

I lift up the bloodstained banner! I lift up Jesus Christ of Nazareth, Jehovah Nissi, my banner and my protector!

I declare Luke 18:1 in the name of Jesus, that I will pray and not faint, and I will not lose heart.

I declare in the name of Jesus Ephesians 6:18. I will continue to pray in the spirit on all occasions, with all kinds of prayers and requests. I declare in the name of Jesus that I will always be alert and that I will always keep on praying for all of the Lord's people.

You said in Your Word, according to Isaiah 65:24, that "before they call, I will answer; while they are still speaking I will hear, says the Lord."

You said in Your Word, in Mark 11:24, that whatever You ask for in prayer, believe that you have received it, and it will be yours.

I believe everything that I am asking You for, God, and I receive it in the name of Jesus!

You said in Matthew 7:7–8, "Ask and it will be given to you; seek and you will find; knock and the door will be opened to you. For everyone who asks receives; he who seeks finds; and to him who knocks, the doors will be opened."

Jesus said in Matthew 18:19–20, "I tell you that if two of you on earth agree about anything you ask for, it will be done for you by my Father in heaven. For where two or three come together in My name, there am I with them."

Therefore, I thank You, heavenly Father, for hearing me each and every time I pray. I thank You for answering me, and I thank You for the supernatural manifestation of Your Word. In Jesus's name. Amen!

# Personalize Your
## Prayers, Decrees & Declarations

# 7

## FAITH
## PROTECTION OVER MY COMMUNITY
## THE WORKS OF MY HANDS
## AND FINANCES

### ADORATION

For You Lord, are good, and ready to forgive, and abundant in lovingkindness to all who call upon You. Give ear, O Lord, to my prayer, and give heed to the voice of my supplication! In the day of my trouble I shall call upon You, for You will answer me. There is no one like You among the gods, O Lord, nor are there any works like Yours. All nations of whom You have made shall come and worship before You, O Lord, any they shall glorify Your name. For You are great and do wondrous deeds. You alone are God (Psalm 86:5–10).

### CONFESSION

Heavenly Father, You said in Your Word, according to 1 John 1:9, if we confess our sins, You are faithful and just to forgive us our sins and to cleanse us from all unrighteousness. God, I'm sorry for falling short in _____ and that my actions in _____ haven't lived up to Your expectations. I

repent for not doing_____ when I should have done_____
. Heavenly Father, I let go of all offense, bitterness, anger, and disappointment, and I release it all unto You. I forgive _____, who have hurt me, disappointed me, and caused me any harm. You said in Your Word to forgive other people when they sin against me so that You, heavenly Father, will also forgive me (Matthew 6:14). I receive Your forgiveness. I have no condemnation in Christ (Romans 8:1), and I thank You for helping me to do better the next time. In Jesus's name. Amen.

## THANKSGIVING

But thanks be to God! He gives us the victory through our Lord Jesus Christ. You are awesome from Your sanctuary. The God of Israel gives strength and power to the people. Blessed Be God (1 Corinthians 15:57; Psalm 67:35)! I thank You dear God for being my Aba Father, God Almighty, The All Sufficient one, the Most High God, and the lifter of my head.

Thank You for being good to me. Thank You for Your mercy, grace, favor and unconditional love that You have shown towards me. Thank You for my life, health and strength. I praise You and I bless Your Holy and Magnificent name. For You are all-knowing, all-powerful, all sufficient, and You are everywhere at the same time.

## SUPPLICATION

## FAITH

I lay hold of my confession of Faith concerning the Word of God, the power of God and our Lord and Savior Jesus Christ. I have faith and trust in You that You are going to do amazing things on my behalf. So be it unto me according to my faith- the substance of things hoped for and the evidence of things not seen (Hebrews 11:1) and Your Infallible Word that does not return back to you void, but accomplishes that which You please, and it shall prosper in the thing whereto You sent it (Isaiah 55:11).

Therefore, I declare in the name of Jesus, Numbers 23:19, For God is not a man, that he should lie, neither the son of man, that he should repent:

hath he said, and shall he not do it? or hath he spoken, and shall he not make it good.

I decree and declare, in the name of Jesus, Job 22:28, thou shalt also decree a thing, and it shall be established unto thee: and the light shall shine upon thy ways. So be it unto me according to Your Word in the name of Jesus.

I call those things that be not, as though they were according to Romans 4:17, concerning my marriage, family, friends, co-workers, ministry, business, finances, leaders and governmental authorities.

I call forth salvation to my family members, friends, co-workers, and to those in governmental authority and leadership positions who are not saved in the name of Jesus.

I call forth peace, unity and reconciliation to my neighborhood and community and areas surrounding me that are experiencing high rates of crime and vandalism.

I speak to the spirits of murder, destruction and mayhem within the jurisdiction that you have given me authority over, and I command these spirits to cease all of its operations and to burn up and die by the Fire of God, in the name of Jesus.

## PROTECTION OVER MY COMMUNITY

I plead the blood of Jesus over my neighborhood and community and declare the safety and protection of the Most High God.

I declare Psalm 91:10–11 in the name of Jesus that no evil shall befall your people, no plague shall come near their dwelling place, and that Your angels are taking charge concerning them and guarding them in all of their ways.

I declare in the name of Jesus that their light will break forth like the dawn, and their healing will quickly appear; their righteousness shall go before them, and their glory is their rear guard (Isaiah 58:8).

I declare in the name of Jesus that You are scattering our enemies before us in seven ways and that they are fleeing now in the name of Jesus Christ of Nazareth (Deuteronomy 28:7).

I declare in the name of Jesus that as I begin to sing and give praises unto God, that You, Jehovah Nissi, are causing confusion on the enemy's camp and that everything that the enemy meant for evil You are turning around for our good (2 Chronicles 20:22; Genesis 50:20).

For You are Almighty God! You love us with an unconditional love, and You care about every intricate detail within our lives.

You said in Your Word that the very hairs of our head are all numbered (Luke 12:7). So, therefore, I declare that I will not fear because I am of more value than many sparrows (Matthew 10:31).

You care about our hopes, plans, dreams, and future. For You said in Your Word that Your plans for me are good, not to harm me but to prosper me and to give me a future and a hope (Jeremiah 29:11).

I thank You for protecting us from danger seen and unseen, evil seen and unseen in the name of Jesus, and that we will not be ignorant of the enemy's devices (2 Corinthians 2:11).

I decree and declare Luke 10:19 in the name of Jesus. You have given us power to tread on serpents and scorpions and over all the power of the enemy, and nothing shall by any means hurt us.

## The Works of My Hands

Father, in the name of Jesus, I call upon you, and I acknowledge how great and amazing You are. You are the great Jehovah, the I AM that I AM. You are Jehovah Jireh, the God of miracles, and the God of increase!

I thank You for creating me in Your image and likeness. For I am the child of the Most High God! I am God's chosen, His elect and most prized possession.

Therefore, I decree and declare blessings over the works of my hands that You have created to be used for Your purposes and for Your glory.

Father, in the name of Jesus, I decree and declare blessings over the works of my hands, to lay hands on the sick so that they shall recover.

I decree and declare in the name of Jesus blessings over the works of my hands, to perform extraordinary miracles, just as You did by the hands of Paul (Acts 19:11–12).

I decree and declare in the name of Jesus blessings over the works of my hands to be anointed and to be used as Your vessel, to impart and administer the baptism of the Holy Spirit (Acts 8:17).

I decree and declare in the name of Jesus blessings over the works of my hands with the anointing and the power of God's Holy Spirit to build up my family, marriage, finances, church, ministry, business, community, city, government, economy, educational system, and public service entities to reflect the image of Almighty God.

I decree and declare in the name of Jesus blessings over the works of my hands to rebuild the ancient ruins, to restore the places long devastated, to renew the ruined cities and the desolations of many generations (Isaiah 61:4).

I decree and declare in the name of Jesus blessings over the works of my hands to pull down strongholds, to actively maneuver the sword of the Spirit, the Word of God, with skill and accuracy, and to cleverly utilize my shield of faith to withstand the schemes and plans of the enemy.

I decree and declare in the name of Jesus blessings over the works of my hands, to be able to uphold my brothers and sisters in love and to bear their burdens (Galatians 6:2).

I decree and declare in the name of Jesus blessings over the works of my hands, to fulfill my God-ordained destiny and to live my life victoriously and in abundance.

## FINANCES

I decree and declare, in the name of Jesus, blessings over my finances in order to help carry out the Great Commission, to spread the Gospel of Jesus Christ and to help advance the kingdom of God.

I decree and declare in the name of Jesus blessings over my finances, to help meet the needs of my brothers and sisters in times of distress, to help the widows and the orphans, those who are homeless, and those who cannot help themselves.

I decree and declare in the name of Jesus Your Word, according to Deuteronomy 15:6, what the Lord has promised: "I shall lend to many nations but will not borrow from none."

I decree and declare in the name of Jesus blessings over my finances to grow, profit, increase, multiply, and flourish, so that I will be able to shower down blessings upon others.

I declare in the name of Jesus that my finances are blessed. I have been young and now am old, yet I have not seen the righteous forsaken, nor his descendants begging bread. He is ever merciful and lends, and his descendants are blessed (Psalm 37:25–26).

I decree and declare Psalm 34:10 in the name of Jesus. The young lions lack and suffer hunger, but those who seek the Lord shall not lack any good thing. I lack no good thing in my God because He is my everything. He is God Almighty. He is the great I AM that I AM!

The Lord is my shepherd, and I shall not want (Psalm 23:1).

The young lions lack and suffer hunger, but those who seek the Lord shall not lack any good thing (Psalm 34:10).

Daily, the Lord loads me with his benefits (Psalm 68:19).

I declare in the name of Jesus that as I walk in the statutes of the Lord and keep His commandments and perform them, He will give me rain in its season, the land shall yield its produce, and the trees of the field shall yield their fruit. My threshing shall last till the time of vintage, and the vintage shall last till the time of sowing. I shall eat my bread to the full and dwell in my land safely (Leviticus 26:3–5).

I declare in the name of Jesus, Job 36:11, as I obey and serve the Lord, I shall spend my days in prosperity and my years in pleasure.

I declare in the name of Jesus, as I continue to love the Lord my God, to walk in His ways, and to keep His commandments, His statutes, and His judgments, that I may live and multiply; the Lord my God will bless me in the land, which I go to possess (Deuteronomy 30:15–16).

For the Lord God is a sun and shield; the Lord will give grace and glory; no good thing will He withhold from those who walk uprightly (Psalm 84:11).

I pray for the peace of Jerusalem: "May they prosper who love you. Peace be within your walls, prosperity within your palaces" (Psalm 122:6–7).

I decree and declare Proverbs 3:9–10. I will Honor the Lord with my possessions, and with the first fruits of all my increase, so my barns will be filled with plenty, and my vats will overflow with new wine.

I decree and declare in the name of Jesus that as I give, it is given back to me in good measure, pressed down, shaken together, and running over, that men shall give into my blossom (Luke 6:38).

Thank You, heavenly Father, for the manifestation of Your Word that says, "Bring the whole tithe into the storehouse, that there may be food in my house. Test me in this," says the LORD Almighty, "and see if I will not throw open the floodgates of heaven and pour out so much blessing that there will not be room enough to store it."

Thank You, heavenly Father, for blessing me according to Your Word as I bring the whole tithes into your storehouse. Thank You, heavenly Father, for rebuking the devour for my sake.

Thank You, heavenly Father, for being the God of miracles and the God of increase (Psalm 77:14; Psalm 115:14). If you can speak this world into existence at the command of Your Word, part the red sea, turn water into wine, feed a multitude of people with five loaves of bread and two pieces of fish, cast out devils, heal the sick, and raise Jesus Christ from the dead, I know and I have total faith and confidence in You to change my financial situation.

Heavenly Father, You said in Your Word that You are Lord, the God of all flesh, and that there is nothing too hard for you to do (Jeremiah 32:27). Heavenly Father, You also said in Your Word, "Ask and it will be given to you; seek and you will find; knock and the door will be opened to you. For everyone who asks receives; the one who seeks finds; and to the one who knocks, the door will be opened" (Matthew 7:7–80). I ask in the name of Jesus for You to renew my mind and help me to be a better steward over my finances. I ask in the name of Jesus for You to help me have a better relationship with You and money.

I ask in the name of Jesus for You to help me think ahead, to be more diligent with my financial planning, and to always take time to consider the cost (Proverbs 13:16; Proverbs 21:5; Luke 14:28).

I ask in the name of Jesus for stable and consistent employment, raises, bonuses, and promotions in order to be able to provide for my family. I also ask in the name of Jesus for the mindset and ability to be able to store up wealth (Proverbs 30:24–25; 1 Timothy 5:8).

Heavenly Father, You said in Your Word that if I am willing and obedient, I shall eat the good of the land (Isaiah 1:19). Here I am, Lord. I am willing to submit to Your will, and I am committed to hear and obey Your Word concerning my finances. You said in Your Word, according to Luke 11:28, but even more blessed are all who hear the Word of God and put it into practice.

Therefore, I repent and ask for Your forgiveness in the name of Jesus, for mishandling money and not being a good steward over finances the way that you have intended it for me.

In the name of Jesus, I break and utterly destroy every generational curse of poverty, lack, and greed over my life and finances! I cancel out every debt and every evil assignment against my finances, in the name of Jesus!

I declare in the name of Jesus that You, Father God, are able to do exceedingly and abundantly above all that I can ask, think, or imagine concerning my financial needs, according to the power that works within me (Ephesians 3:20–21).

For You are the Lord God that supplies all of my needs according to Your riches and glory in Christ Jesus (Philippians 4:19).

I thank You, Father God, that You make all grace abound toward me with all sufficiency, so that I will have abundance for every good work (2 Corinthians 9:8).

I declare an increase and supernatural influx of wealth in the name of Jesus, to be a blessing to others and to help advance the kingdom of God.

I declare Deuteronomy 28:12, that the Lord will open for me His good storehouse, the heavens, to give rain to my land in its season and to bless all the work of my hand, and I shall lend to many nations, but I shall not borrow.

I declare in the name of Jesus that I am blessed because I fear the Lord and take delight in His commandments. I am the generation of the upright, and I am blessed. Wealth and riches are in my house, and my righteousness in Christ Jesus endures forever (Psalm 112:1–3).

For the God of heaven will give me success (Nehemiah 2:20). I am like a tree firmly planted by the streams of water, which yields its fruit in its season, and its leaf does not wither, and whatever I do, I prosper, in Jesus's name (Psalm 1:3).

In the name of Jesus, I declare Psalm 92:12. I am righteous, and I shall flourish like the palm tree; I shall grow like a cedar in Lebanon.

Surely, the Lord will set me high above all the nations of the earth. Blessings are coming upon me and overtaking me. Blessed shall I be in the city, and blessed shall I be in the country. Blessed shall be the offspring of my body and the produce of my ground and the offspring of my beasts, the increase of my herd and the young of my flock. Blessed shall be my basket and my kneading bowl. Blessed shall I be when I come in, and blessed shall I be when I go out. For the Lord God will cause my enemies who rise up against me to be defeated before me; they will come out against me one way and will flee before me seven ways (Deuteronomy 28:1–7).

For the Lord gives me increase, me and my children. I declare in the name of Jesus I am blessed of the Lord, the maker of heaven and earth. The heavens are the heavens of the Lord, but the earth He has given to the sons of men, and that includes me (Psalm 115:14–16).

I declare in the name of Jesus Your favor upon my life. I declare Psalm 5:12; surely, Lord, You bless me, the righteous. You surround me with favor as with a shield.

For You are a supernatural God. You can cause men, women, and children to give into my bosom.

Thank You, heavenly Father, for giving me the power to make wealth (Deuteronomy 8:18). I thank You, Lord, for teaching me how to profit in the name of Jesus (Isaiah 48:7).

Thank You, Lord, that the wealth of the wicked is being supernaturally released to me, the righteous (Proverbs 13:22). I receive the wealth laid up for me in Jesus's name.

I declare in the name of Jesus the blessings of the Lord upon my life are making me rich, and it adds no sorrow with it (Proverbs 10:22).

For You are a supernatural God, and there is nothing too hard for you to do (Jeremiah 32:27).

You are able to do exceedingly, abundantly above all than I can ask or think according to the power that works within me, and I thank You for it (Ephesians 3:20).

I bless Your holy name. Thank you for being a supernatural God! Thank you for causing everything to work together for my good, because I love you, and I am called according to Your purpose (Romans 8:28).

I declare in the name of Jesus that as I continue to be faithful in the little things, You Father God, will make me ruler over many (Luke 16:10).

I will not despise the day of small beginnings (Zechariah 4:10). For You choose the foolish things of the world to confound the wise and the weak things of the world to shame the strong (1 Corinthians 1:27). For I am the head and not the tail, above only and not beneath (Deuteronomy 28:13). You said in Your Word the last shall be first and the first last; for many are called but few are chosen (Matthew 20:16). I thank You for choosing me for such a time as this, and I thank You for taking me into a wealthy place and that of abundance. Nothing missing and nothing lacking. I trust You, Father God, and I thank You for fulfilling every promise in my life according to Your Word and within this prayer. In Jesus's name. Amen.

# *Personalize Your*
## *Prayers, Decrees & Declarations*

---- DAY ----

# 8

## DECLARING THE WORD OF GOD
## EXERCISING MY FAITH, POWER, AND AUTHORITY IN GOD FOR HEALING AND DELIVERANCE
## DECLARING BLESSINGS, SAFETY, AND PROTECTION OVER PEOPLE

### ADORATION

Jesus, I worship You for who You are. You are the Alpha and the Omega. You are the Who Is and Who Is to come, the Almighty. You are the lion of the tribe of Judah. You are holy. You are righteous, just, and true. There is nobody like You. Worthy is the lamb that was slain to receive power and riches and wisdom and might and honor and glory and blessing. To Him who sits on the throne and to the lamb be blessing and honor and glory and dominion forever and ever (Revelation 8:1; Revelation 5:5; Revelation 5:12–13).

## Confession

Heavenly Father, You said in Your Word, according to 1 John 1:9, if we confess our sins, You are faithful and just to forgive us our sins and to cleanse us from all unrighteousness. God, I'm sorry for falling short in _____ and that my actions in _____ haven't lived up to Your expectations. I repent for not doing_____ when I should have done_____. Heavenly Father, I let go of all offense, bitterness, anger, and disappointment, and I release it all unto You. I forgive _____, who have hurt me, disappointed me, and caused me any harm. You said in Your Word to forgive other people when they sin against me so that You, heavenly Father, will also forgive me (Matthew 6:14). I receive Your forgiveness. I have no condemnation in Christ (Romans 8:1), and I thank You for helping me to do better the next time. In Jesus's name. Amen.

## Thanksgiving

Father, in the name of Jesus, I thank You for another day and for the privilege to come into Your presence to pray, intercede, and to make bold declarations according to Your Word in faith, in confidence, with your anointing, and with the power of Your Holy Spirit.

What a privilege and honor to be able to dwell in Your presence! For in Your presence there is the fullness of joy, liberty, peace, safety, protection, and rest (2 Corinthians 3:17; Philippians 4:7; Psalm 16:11; Psalm 91:1–16; Matthew 11:29). He who dwells in the shelter of the Most High (meaning the blessings for believers who habitually reside and fellowship in God's presence—the inner sanctuary, the mercy seat, and the most holy place where there is refuge, peace, love, joy, safety, and protection) will abide in the shadow of the Almighty (Psalm 91:1).

For Your Word says in Revelation 21:3, "And I heard a loud voice from the throne saying, behold, the dwelling place of God is with man. He will dwell with them, and they will be His people, and God himself will be with them as their God."

I thank You for being Jehovah Shammah, the God who is *always* there (Ezekiel 48:35; Revelations 21–22). For the Lord my God will always go with me; He will never leave me or forsake me (Deuteronomy 31:6).

## SUPPLICATION

## DECLARING THE WORD OF GOD

Your holy Word is with me.

You have written Your Word on my heart, and Your Word dwells in me richly with all wisdom (Colossians 3:16).

I come in agreement with the Word of God and the Spirit of God, and I declare in the name of Jesus that You have given me power in my tongue to speak life and death (Proverbs 18:21).

I declare in the name of Jesus that I will continue to use the Word of God to speak life and to utterly destroy the forces of darkness.

## EXERCISING MY FAITH, POWER, AND AUTHORITY IN GOD FOR HEALING AND DELIVERANCE

With the Word of God and the releasing of my faith, I exercise my power, authority, and dominion in Jesus Christ.

I speak life to my mortal body, and I speak life to those around me who are battling sickness and disease.

I speak to sickness and disease and declare that it cannot stay in my body, in the name of Jesus.

I declare in the name of Jesus that my body is the temple of the Holy Spirit (1 Corinthians 6:19–20).

I declare in the name of Jesus that I will not die but live and tell of the works of the Lord (Psalm 118:17).

For You came to give me life, and life more than abundantly, in the name of Jesus (John 10:10).

I use my tongue to speak, decree, declare, and take authority over the spirit of infirmity, in the name of Jesus.

I command sickness, disease, stroke, cancer, diabetes, heart problems, cardiovascular disease, and high blood pressure to bow down at the name of Jesus.

I cast out the spirit of inheritance of stroke and the death of brain cells, in the name of Jesus. I speak to the brain and command all blockage to dissolve and be removed. I command all damaged tissue to be restored in the name of Jesus. I command a creative miracle and a new brain in the name of Jesus.

I bind and cast out the spirit of cancer in the name of Jesus. I curse the seed, root, and cells of cancer in the name of Jesus. I speak to every affected area within my body, and I command every cancer cell in my body to dry up and die in the name of Jesus. I command the bone marrow to produce pure, healthy blood in the name of Jesus. I command healing in the name of Jesus to all organs and tissues affected and restoration to every part of the body where it needs to be restored in the name of Jesus. I declare in the name of Jesus for every good cell within my body to seek out and destroy every bad cell. I command the body's defensive killer cells to multiply and attack every cancer cell in the name of Jesus.

I speak to diabetes, and I cast out the spirits of inheritance in the name of Jesus.

I command and speak forth a new pancreas into my body in the name of Jesus. I command any damaged parts of my body due to excess sugar to be healed, restored, and made whole in the name of Jesus!

I speak to cardiovascular disease and heart problems in the name of Jesus. I speak a new heart into my body, and I command a creative miracle in the name of Jesus. I speak to my arms, and I command my arms to grow out and for all other parts of my body affected by heart disease to be healed in the name of Jesus.

High blood pressure, I speak to you in the name of Jesus. I command a divine roto-rooter treatment throughout the entire vascular system in the name of Jesus.

I command the blood pressure to return to normal and to remain normal in the name of Jesus.

I declare in the name of Jesus and by the power of God's Holy spirit a creative miracle within my body.

I speak to every organ, every tissue, and every cell within my body, and I command it to be healed and to line up according to the Word of God in the name of Jesus!

I command the electrical and chemical frequency within my body to be in perfect harmony, balance, and alignment, in the name of Jesus.

I command every bone, tendon, muscle, and joint within my body to be strengthened and lengthened in the name of Jesus. I command all pain to go away, disappear, and to be thou removed and cast into the sea, never to return again in the name of Jesus. Wherever there is any misalignment in my arms and legs, I speak forth a creative miracle. I command my arms and legs to grow out and to be in perfect alignment in the name of Jesus.

I command my immune systems to be strong, healthy, and vibrant and to function normally in the name of Jesus.

I thank You, Father, that You satisfy my mouth with good things so that my youth is being renewed like an eagle's (Psalm 103:5).

Daily, You load my mouth with benefits (Psalm 68:19). For Your Word is life to those who find them and health to one's whole body (Proverbs 4:22).

I thank You that there is no distance in the spirit. You sent Your Word to heal me and to deliver me from all destruction (Psalm 107:20).

You also said that Your Word does not return unto You void without accomplishing what You have desired and without succeeding in the matter for which You sent it, which is to heal, restore, save, deliver, set free, and utterly destroy the works and plans of the enemy (Isaiah 55:11). So be it unto me according to Your Word when I decree it, declare it, say it, and pray it in the name of Jesus!

The angels of the Lord are harkening to the voice of Your Word (Psalm 103:20).

Your power follows Your Word, and it is manifesting the presence of the Holy Spirit on the inside of me, and the devil's ailments of sickness and disease are fleeing from me now in the name of Jesus.

I declare in the name of Jesus that Your Word and Your presence are setting me free from demonic oppression, possession. Your Word and Your presence are setting me free from depression and healing and delivering my body and my mind, and I am set free in the name of Jesus!

For whom the son sets free is free in deed in the name of Jesus (John 8:36). Hallelujah! I declare that I am free for real because of the shed blood of Jesus Christ.

I am the redeemed of the Lord (Psalm 107:2). I have been redeemed from the curse of the law, which is poverty, sickness, and death. It was for freedom that Christ set me free, and therefore I will continue to stand firm and will not be subject to a yoke of slavery (Galatians 5:1).

Thank You for the ultimate price You paid for my life, and because You laid down Your life for me and went to the Father, I have the Holy Spirit!

I declare in the name of Jesus that I have the anointing and the power of God's Holy Spirit to speak, decree, and declare miracles. Your Word says in Job 22:28 that I shall also decree a thing, and it shall be established unto me, and the light shall shine on my ways.

I decree and declare in the name of Jesus that as a living epistle, I will let my light shine before others so that they may see my good deeds and glorify my Father in heaven (Matthew 5:16).

I declare in the name of Jesus that I am strong and will do mighty exploits because I know my God (Daniel 11:32).

I am a child of the Most High God, and I am Abraham's seed and an heir according to the promise (Galatians 3:29)!

I thank You, heavenly Father, that You have bestowed upon me and within me Your Word, authority, anointing, and the power of Your Holy Spirit.

I declare in the name of Jesus that I will operate in love and unity. I will operate in the supernatural anointing and the power of God's Holy Spirit to perform miracles, signs, and wonders of healing and deliverance so that the unbeliever, the lost, and the wicked will believe, repent, and accept Jesus Christ as their Lord and Savior.

## DECLARING BLESSINGS, SAFETY, AND PROTECTION OVER PEOPLE

Father, in the name of Jesus, I declare the Beatitudes over Your people as it is written in Matthew 5:3–12:

> Blessed are the poor in spirit, for theirs is the kingdom of heaven.
> Blessed are those who mourn, for they shall be comforted.
> Blessed are the gentle, for they shall inherit the earth.
> Blessed are those who hunger and thirst for righteousness, for they shall be satisfied.
> Blessed are the merciful, for they shall receive mercy.
> Blessed are the pure in heart, for they shall see God.
> Blessed are the peacemakers, for they shall be called sons of God.
> Blessed are those who have been persecuted for the sake of righteousness, for theirs is the kingdom of heaven.
> Blessed are you when people insult you and persecute you, and falsely say all kinds of evil against you because of Me.

Rejoice and be glad, for your reward in heaven is great; for in the same way they persecuted the prophets who were before you.

I declare in the name of Jesus that I am a lender and not a borrower (Deuteronomy 28:12). Therefore, I will use what You have given me to be a blessing to Your people and especially to the orphan and the widow.

Your Word says in James 1:27 that pure, undefiled religion in the sight of our God and Father is "to visit orphans and widows in their distress, and to keep oneself unstained by the world."

For You have called me in such a time as this to pray, help, and defend the orphan and the widow.

Father, in the name of Jesus, I lift up to You every widow and every child in foster care this morning. I know that You are a father to the fatherless and a mother to the motherless. You said in Your Word that you will never leave us or forsake us (Deuteronomy 31:6). So be it unto those who are without their parents, family, and loved ones, according to Your Word, in Jesus's name.

Father, in the name of Jesus, I declare a hedge of protection around every widow and orphan today. I ask in the name of Jesus for You to cover them in Your precious blood, Your presence, Your power, and Your peace. Station Your heavenly angels around them and protect them from danger seen and unseen, evil seen and unseen, in the name of Jesus. I declare healing in their hearts, minds, and physical body from abuse, neglect, sexual exploitation, sexual abuse, and trauma. There is no distance in the Spirit. You are God Almighty, and You sent Your Word and healed them and delivered them from all destruction in the name of Jesus (Psalm 107:20).

I declare that everything that the enemy meant for evil You are turning around for their good because You are an amazing and awesome God (Genesis 50:20).

I thank You for being a very present help in their time of trouble and that You are sending forth Your divine laborers to intervene and help them spiritually, physically, and mentally.

Thank You, heavenly Father, for sending your angelic aid to their rescue.

Thank You, Jehovah Mephalti, for delivering them from the hands of the enemy (Luke 1:71–74).

I declare that no weapon formed against them shall prosper in the name of Jesus (Isaiah 54:17).

I bind up the spirit of fear in the name of Jesus, and I loose forth the everlasting saving Word of God. I declare in the name of Jesus that you did not give them a spirit of fear but of power, love, and a sound mind (2 Timothy 1:7).

I declare in the name of Jesus that they shall have peace, rest, and a sound mind in You.

I give You all glory and honor and praise! I thank You for the supernatural manifestation of Your Word within this decree, declaration, and prayer. In Jesus's name. Amen.

# Personalize Your
## Prayers, Decrees & Declarations

PERSONAL ENCOURAGEMENT

SPIRITUAL WARFARE

BLESSINGS

HEALING AND PROTECTION

MINISTERING SALVATION

PRAYER FOR FAMILY MEMBERS

## ADORATION

Father, in the name of Jesus, what a privilege and honor to be in Your presence this morning. I thank You for being an amazing, awesome, and magnificent God. For You are the Lord God Almighty, and Your kingdom reigns forever and ever. I love You, I appreciate You, and I adore You.

## CONFESSION

Heavenly Father, You said in Your Word, according to 1 John 1:9, if we confess our sins, You are faithful and just to forgive us our sins and to cleanse us from all unrighteousness. God, I'm sorry for falling short in _____ and that my actions in _____ haven't lived up to Your expectations. I repent for not doing_____ when I should have done_____ . Heavenly Father, I let go of all offense, bitterness, anger, and disappointment, and I release it all unto You. I forgive _____, who have hurt me, disappointed me, and caused me any harm. You said in Your Word to forgive other people when they sin against me so that You, heavenly Father, will also forgive me (Matthew 6:14). I receive Your forgiveness. I have no condemnation in Christ (Romans 8:1), and I thank You for helping me to do better the next time. In Jesus's name. Amen.

## THANKSGIVING

Father, in the name of Jesus, I thank You that Your eyes are toward the righteous and Your ears attend to our prayers. Thank You for the power of Your Holy Spirit that dwells within me and for the manifestation of Your Holy Word being evident in my life.

## SUPPLICATION

### PERSONAL ENCOURAGEMENT

I declare the Word of God, according to Psalm 18:31–36, "For you are the God alone who is a rock, who girds me with strength and makes my ways blameless. You make my feet like hinds' feet, and You set me upon high places. You train my hands for battle, so that my arms can bend a bow of bronze. You have given me the shield of Your salvation and Your right hand upholds us. Your gentleness makes me great and You enlarge my steps under me, and my feet have not slipped."

I take courage in Your great name and draw strength from Your Word.

It is in You that I live, move, and have my being (Acts 17:28).

I am strong in You, Lord, and in the power of Your might (Ephesians 6:10)!

I am more than a conqueror through Jesus Christ, who loved me (Romans 8:37)!

I take ground, I take territory, and I use the power and authority that

God has given me to take the land and occupy until You return in the name of Jesus (Luke 19:13).

I take authority over the enemy in the name of Jesus, and I declare that for this reason the son of God was manifested that He might destroy the works of the devil and that the works of the devil are destroyed (1 John 3:8).

## SPIRITUAL WARFARE

I declare in the name of Jesus that the works of the enemy are destroyed! The works of the enemy are destroyed over my life, over my health and strength, over my finances, over my marriage, and over my relationships, children, grandchildren, family members, employment, and ministry in the name of Jesus!

I declare in the name of Jesus that the enemy is under my feet, and I will open up my mouth and declare the Word of God and act on the Word of God to keep him there.

For You have given me authority to tread on serpents and scorpions and over all the power of the enemy, and nothing shall injure me (Luke 10:19).

For the weapons of my warfare are not carnal but mighty through God to the pulling down of strongholds (2 Corinthians 10:4).

You have given me the power to bind and to loose, according to Mathew 18:18. For whatever I bind on earth shall have been bound in heaven, and whatever I loose on earth shall have been loosed in heaven.

Therefore, I bind up drug and alcohol addiction, the spirits of fear, depression, pride, strife, discord, hate, jealousy, racism, retaliation, false religion, lawlessness, rebellion, falling away from the faith, anxiety, mental illnesses, infirmities, sorcery, witchcraft, hexes, spells, voodoo, the accuser of the brethren, the spirit of Jezebel, and the spirit of Absalom in the jurisdiction that you have given me authority over in the name of Jesus.

I loose forth the Word of God in the name of Jesus.

I declare in the name of Jesus that no weapon formed against me shall prosper and every tongue that rises against me in judgment I shall condemn (Isaiah 54:17).

I declare in the name of Jesus that no man can curse whom God has blessed (Numbers 23:20). I am the generation of the upright, and I declare the Word of God, that the generation of the upright shall be blessed (Psalm 112:2).

## Blessings

Blessed be the God and Father of our Lord Jesus Christ, who has blessed me with every spiritual blessing in the heavenly places in Christ, according to Ephesians 1:3, in the name of Jesus.

I declare Psalm 128:5 in the name of Jesus. The Lord blesses me from Zion, and I shall see the prosperity of Jerusalem (the foundation of peace) all the days of my life.

I declare Ezekiel 34:26 in the name of Jesus. The Lord will make me and the places around His hill a blessing, and the Lord will cause showers to come down in my season, and I shall be showers of blessing.

For this is my season and year of supernatural favor, blessings, and overflow! Therefore, I declare in the name of Jesus that God is showering His blessings upon me and that I will be showering down blessings upon others in the name of Jesus!

I thank You, Father God, for Your divine favor and for causing me to be a generous person. According to Proverbs 11:25, the generous man will be prosperous, and he who waters will himself be watered.

I declare in the name of Jesus that You are positioning and setting me up to give and to sow into good ground and in order to help every widow, orphan, those who are in prison, those who are homeless, and those who are in great need during a parched time such as this. I declare in the name of Jesus that I will receive a hundredfold return on what I have already sown and will continue to sow.

I declare these showers of blessings to overflow in every area of my life—spiritually, physically, emotionally, and financially—in the name of Jesus.

Holy Spirit, let Your blessings and living waters flow—overflow in my ministry, gifts, talents, home, family, marriage, finances, and business. Holy Spirit, overflow in my personal relationship with You and my walk with You.

I declare an overflow of healing in the physical and mental ailments of my bod, and an overflow in ministering deliverance and setting all those who are bound free in the name of Jesus.

I declare an overflow in my finances and employment in the name of Jesus.

I declare new business opportunities and job promotions in the name of Jesus.

I declare new housing from You, Lord, in the name of Jesus.

I declare Malachi 3:11, that you are opening up the windows of heaven and are pouring out a blessing upon me until it overflows in the name of Jesus!

I declare in the name of Jesus that the wealth of the wicked is being released to the just and that it is being released to me (the just) in an overflow, in the name of Jesus.

I declare in the name of Jesus that from out of my belly, there shall be a flow of living streams of waters (John 7:38). I declare in the name of Jesus that You are continually overflowing and filling my mouth with Your Word. I declare in the name of Jesus an overflow of Your Holy Spirit, an overflow of Your presence, an overflow of Your power, an overflow of Your peace, an overflow of Your love, and that You are overflowing and filling me with Your unspeakable joy!

With that, I declare a supernatural overflow of showers of blessings upon me and that there will be a supernatural overflow of showers of blessings to others in this year, with astonishment and a supernatural abundance of Your favor overtaking me. In the name of Jesus!

## HEALING AND PROTECTION

I thank You for my healing and that the works of the enemy are destroyed!

Healing is the children's bread in the name of Jesus (Matthew 15:22–28; Mark 7:24–30)!

I declare that I am the healed and not the sick in the name of Jesus.

I command sickness and disease leave my body in the name of Jesus. Depression must go from me in the name of Jesus, and every unclean foul spirit that is trying to manifest itself upon me, my children, marriage, family, coworkers, friends, and relationships—I command it to go now, in the name of Jesus!

In the name of Jesus, I declare Isaiah 53:5, that Jesus Christ was wounded for my transgressions and bruised for my inequities, and the chastisement of my peace was upon Him, and by His stripes I am healed (Isaiah 53:5).

You sent Your Word to heal me and to deliver me from my destruction (Psalm 107:20).

For many are the afflictions of the righteous, but the Lord, Jehovah Mephalti, You deliver me out of them all (Psalm 34:19).

I declare in the name of Jesus that no plague shall come near my dwelling places and that the angels of the Lord are taking charge concerning me and are guarding me in all of my ways (Psalm 91:10–11).

Therefore, I will not be afraid of the terror by night, of the arrow that flies by day, of the pestilence that stalks in darkness, or of the destruction that lays waste at noon, in the name of Jesus (Psalm 91:5–6).

You said in Your Word that one thousand may fall at my side, and ten thousand at my right hand, but it (no plague, no sickness, no disease, no hurt, no harm, no danger) shall not approach me in the name of Jesus (Psalm 91:7).

You did not give me the spirit of fear but of power, love, and a sound mind in the name of Jesus (1 Timothy 1:7).

I declare Psalm 27:1–2, "For the Lord is my light and my salvation, for whom shall I fear? He is the defense of my life, whom shall I dread? For when evildoers came upon me to devour my flesh, my adversaries and my enemies, they stumbled and fell." Therefore, let God arise and my enemies be scattered in the name of Jesus (Psalm 68:1)!

I bind and rebuke every evil plan, plot, and scheme of the enemy to kill, steal, and destroy in my life, in the name of Jesus. For You came to give me life and life more abundantly (John 10:10)!

I declare in the name of Jesus that I shall see the goodness of the Lord in the land of the living (Psalm 27:13).

You will rebuke the devour for my sake in the name of Jesus (Malachi 3:11).

For if You are for me, You are more than the whole world who is against me (Romans 8:31).

Greater is He who is in me than He who is in the world (1 John 4:4)!

The same power that raised Jesus Christ from the dead is within me (Romans 8:11)!

I am the righteousness of God in Christ Jesus (2 Corinthians 5:21). I am a child of the Most High God (Galatians 3:26–29). I am a child of the light, the generation of the upright, the apple of God's eye, the salt of the earth, and I will rejoice and be glad about it (1 Thessalonians 5:5; Psalm 112:2; Psalm 17:8; Matthew 5:13)!

For the gates of hell will not and shall not prevail against me (Matthew 16:18)!

You fight for me, and all I need to do is keep still (Exodus 14:14).

You contend with those who contend with me (Isaiah 49:25).

Because You never lose a battle, I never lose a battle! For you are the king of glory, Jehovah the Lord, strong and mighty in battle (Psalm 24:8).

My victory is certain in You. Thanks be unto God, who gives me the victory and always causes me to triumph (1 Corinthians 15:57)!

I overcome by the blood of the lamb and by the word of my testimony in the name of Jesus (Revelation 12:11).

I press toward the goal for the prize of the upward call of God in Christ Jesus (Philippians 3:14).

Your plans for me are good, plans not to harm me but to prosper me and to give me a hope and a future (Jeremiah 29:11)! For this reason, I declare in the name of Jesus that I am walking by faith and not by sight (2 Corinthians 5:7)!

I know that You are perfecting everything that concerns me, and You are causing everything to work together for my good because I love you and am called according to Your purpose (Romans 8:28)!

## MINISTERING SALVATION

I thank You, Lord, for using me for such a time as this, to help carry out Your purpose and plan of salvation for those who are lost and not saved.

I declare in the name of Jesus that as I walk as a child of the light, I will keep my light lit with the oil of the anointing and the power of Your Holy Spirit, love and compassion, so that Your presence rests and remains upon me and in me to be a powerful witness.

I declare that as I lift up the name of Jesus, people will be drawn unto You. They will confess, believe, and receive Jesus Christ as their Lord and Savior (John 12:32; Romans 10:9–10).

## Prayer for Family Members

I lift up to You my family this day, and I declare healing, peace, restoration, and salvation.

I declare a hedge of protection around them in the name of Jesus.

I declare that it is well with my family and that You are looking ahead and making provision for them because You are Jehovah Jireh (Luke 12:24). You are omniscient, all-knowing, omnipotent, all-powerful, and omnipresent. You are everywhere at the same time.

I declare in the name of Jesus You are going before them to make every crooked place in their life straight and every rough place smooth (Isaiah 45:2–7).

I declare in the name of Jesus that You are ordering their steps and You will not let their foot slip (Psalm 37:23; Psalm 121:3).

I declare Psalm 121:3 over my family, "He will not suffer thy foot to be moved (God will not allow any evil to approach them, so as to do them hurt) and He that keepeth thee will not slumber nor sleep (His vigilance is unceasing)."

Your Word says in Psalm 37:23 that the steps of a righteous man are ordered by the Lord, and He delights in His way. I thank You, Lord, for ordering the steps of every family member in the name of Jesus!

I thank You that my family will not walk in the council of the wicked, or set foot on the path of sinners, or sit in the seat of mockers. I declare in the name of Jesus that my family's delight will be in the delight of the Lord, and in His law they meditate day and night. They shall be like a tree firmly planted by streams of water, yielding its fruit in its season, whose leaf does not wither, and whatever they do, they shall prosper in the name of Jesus (Psalm 1:1–3).

I declare in the name of Jesus, year after year, they will be astonished, wonderstruck, flabbergasted, and amazed by God's supernatural favor and the overflow of God's showers of blessings, so that they will be able to supernaturally overflow with showers of blessings onto others (Ezekiel 34:26).

Hallelujah. I bless Your holy name!

For You are the Great Jehovah, and I give You all of the glory, the honor, and the praise!

For You alone are worthy to be praised! Thank You for hearing and answering this prayer. In Jesus's name. Amen.

# Personalize Your
## Prayers, Decrees & Declarations

INTERCESSION WITH OTHER BELIEVERS
LEADERS AND GOVERNMENTAL
AUTHORITY
PRAYER FOR OUR SPIRITUAL LEADERS
THE BODY OF CHRIST, PRAYER,
DECREES, AND DECLARATION
FOR FAMILY MEMBERS, FRIENDS,
CHILDREN, AND UNSAVED LOVED ONES
TARGETED PRAYERS AND
DECLARATIONS FOR OUR CHILDREN
SPIRITUAL WARFARE PRAYERS
AND DECLARATIONS

## ADORATION

O clap your hands, all people. Shout to God with a voice of Joy. For the Lord Most High is to be feared. A great king over all the earth (Psalm 47:1–2). God reigns over the nations. God sits on His holy throne. You are a good God. You are great, You are holy, and I love You. Let the sea resound and all that fills it; let the fields exult and all that is in them (1 Chronicles 16:33). For You are the only true and living God.

## CONFESSION

Heavenly Father, You said in Your Word, according to 1 John 1:9, if we confess our sins, You are faithful and just to forgive us our sins and to cleanse us from all unrighteousness. God, I'm sorry for falling short in _____ and that my actions in _____ haven't lived up to Your expectations. I repent for not doing_____ when I should have done_____ . Heavenly Father, I let go of all offense, bitterness, anger, and disappointment, and I release it all unto You. I forgive _____, who have hurt me, disappointed me, and caused me any harm. You said in Your Word to forgive other people when they sin against me so that You, heavenly Father, will also forgive me (Matthew 6:14). I receive Your forgiveness. I have no condemnation in Christ (Romans 8:1), and I thank You for helping me to do better the next time. In Jesus's name. Amen.

## THANKSGIVING

I thank You for our time together on this day as I stand in the gap, pray, and intercede with bold declarations and decrees on behalf of leaders, my nation, and others.

As I go forth in prayer, I thank You that You are with me.

Lord, I thank You for fellowship and communion with You.

I thank You for my partnership with You and that You hear me each and every time I come before your throne to pray.

I thank You that You always come through for me each and every time I pray and declare Your Word.

Where the Word of a king is, there is power (Ecclesiastes 8:4).

Therefore, as kings and as Your royal priesthood, I release Your holy Word.

You said in Your Word if any man speak, let him speak as the oracles of God; if any man minister, let him do it as of the ability that God giveth, that

God in all things may be glorified through Jesus Christ, to whom be praise and dominion for ever and ever (1 Peter 4:11).

I thank You that Your Word will not return to you empty without accomplishing what you desire and without succeeding in the matter for which You sent it (Isaiah 55:11).

I thank You, God, that You are not a man, that You should lie, nor a son of man, that You should repent. "Has He said, and will He not do it? Or has He spoken, and will He not make it good?" (Numbers 23:19).

I thank You, God, that You hasten to Your Word to perform it (Jeremiah 1:12).

I bless You Lord for your angels that excel in strength, that do Your commandments, that hearken unto the voice of Your Word (Psalm 103:20).

For this is the confidence I have before the Lord, that if I ask anything according to His will, He hears me. And if I know that He hears me in whatever I ask. I know that I have the requests that I have asked from Him (1 John 5:14–15).

## SUPPLICATION

### INTERCESSION WITH OTHER BELIEVERS

I thank You for unity and uplifted hearts as I pray and intercede with other born-again believers. Your Word says in Ecclesiastes 4:9–10 that two people are better off than one, for they can help each other succeed, and if either of them falls down, one can help the other up.

I thank You, Lord, that the effectual fervent prayer of the righteous are availing much (James 5:16).

I declare in the name of Jesus that we are taking ground and taking territory because we are praying with all prayer and petition, and we are praying at all times in the Spirit, and we are alert with all perseverance and petition for all the saints (Ephesians 6:18).

I thank You, Lord, that iron is sharpening iron as one man sharpens another (Isaiah 27:17) and that Yokes are being destroyed and burdens are being lifted by the anointing of God and the power of Your Holy Spirit.

For Your Word says in Isaiah 10:27 that the yoke shall be destroyed because of the anointing of God.

We thank You that we are God's *poiema*—His creative masterpiece in

Christ Jesus, for good works to operate in the supernatural, to preach the Gospel, minister salvation, cast out devils, heal the sick, raise the dead, and transform, impact, empower, and equip every born-again believer and unbeliever.

For we are a chosen people, a royal priesthood, a holy nation, God's special possession, that you may declare the praises of him who called you out of darkness into his wonderful light (1 Peter 2:9).

We thank You for allowing us to be a part of Your plan and for giving us an ear to hear what the spirit of the Lord has to say as we listen as disciples, the Christian Church of the Living God (Revelation 2:29; Revelation 3:22).

## Prayer for Leaders and Governmental Authority

Lord, I lift up to You our government and those who are in leadership and authority over this nation. I speak the peace of God to their hearts, their minds, and their spirits.

I declare in the name of Jesus that You will keep them and their families in perfect peace.

I declare in the name of Jesus that You will give them wisdom and a sound mind to make the appropriate decisions in order to keep our country safe and to protect the well-being of every citizen in a fair and just manner.

I declare Philippians 2:4 in the name of Jesus that they will look out not merely for their own personal interests but also for the interests of others.

I pray for every unsaved leader in authority of this nation and country. I declare in the name of Jesus that You will send forth divine laborers across their path to be witnesses to them about our Lord and Savior, Jesus Christ. I pray for their hearts to be softened, their ears to be attentive, and for their spirits to be ready to receive the gift of salvation.

You said in Your Word that it is good and acceptable in Your sight for us to pray for our earthly leaders and those who are in authority over us.

Your Word tells us in 1 Timothy 2:1–4 that you urge that entreaties, prayers, petitions, and thanksgivings be made on behalf of all men, for kings and all who are in authority, so that we may lead a tranquil and quiet life in all godliness and dignity. For this is acceptable in the sight of God, our Savior. For you desire all people to be saved and to come to the knowledge of the truth.

I declare in the name of Jesus that our leaders and those who are in governmental authority shall know the truth, and the truth shall set them free (John 8:32).

## Prayer for Our Spiritual Leaders

Father, not only do we lift up our earthly leader, but we also lift up to you our spiritual leaders. We lift up to you (name your spiritual leaders).

I declare a hedge of protection around them, and I plead the blood of Jesus over them.

I declare Psalm 91:1, 10, 11 over my spiritual leaders, which states, "He who dwells in the shelter of the Most High God will abide in the shadow of the almighty. No evil shall befall them, nor no will any plague come near their dwelling places. For He will give his angels charge concerning them to guard them in all of their ways."

I declare in the name of Jesus that You are causing everything to work together for their good because they love You and are called according to Your purpose. I thank You for meeting every one of their needs (Romans 8:28; Philippians 4:19).

For You are Jehovah Jireh, our God who supplies all of our needs according to Your riches and glory in the name of Jesus (Philippians 4:19).

They lack no good thing in you (Psalm 23:1).

You are able to do exceedingly abundantly above all that we ask or think according to the power that works within us (Ephesians 3:20).

You are a good God!

You always look ahead and make provision for them!

You are Jehovah Rehoboth, and You are opening doors for them that no man may shut, in the name of Jesus.

I declare in the name of Jesus that God is making all grace abound toward them so that they may have all sufficiency in all things and an abundance for every good work (2 Corinthians 9:8).

## Prayer and Declarations for the Body of Christ

Father in the name of Jesus, I lift up to You the body of Christ and their families.

I declare that their minds remain fixed on You and that You are keeping them in perfect peace. You said in Your Word that you will keep us in perfect peace, those whose mind is stayed on Thee (Isaiah 26:3).

I declare that You are the lifter of their head. You are causing Your face to shine upon them, You uphold them with Your righteous right hand, and You are looking ahead and making provision for them (Psalm 3:3; Numbers 6:25; Isaiah 41:10; Genesis 22:14).

I declare in the name of Jesus that everything that they stand in need of, whether it be a job, a promotion, housing, success in school, success for their business, success for their ministry, or for a wayward child to come home, every need is met according to Your Word in the name of Jesus. For You are the God who supplies all of our needs according to your riches and glory in Christ Jesus (Genesis 22:14; Philippians 4:19)!

## Prayer and Declaration for Family Members, Friends, Children, and Unsaved Loved Ones

I call out our family members, children, friends, and unsaved loved ones who are caught up in the world, the deception of the world, the lust of the flesh, the lust of the eyes, and the pride of life.

I call them out of the streets and out of abusive situations in the name of Jesus!

I cast out the spirit of drug addiction and its inheritance, in the name of Jesus, and I curse it from their generational bloodline in the name of Jesus! I speak to the spirit of drug addiction and alcoholism, and I rebuke it in the name of Jesus and command it to go back to the pits of hell of where it came from and never return upon them again, in Jesus's name. I bind it up in the name of Jesus! I bind up the spirit of every drug addiction and alcoholism in the name of Jesus that has come upon our children and family members—meth, fentanyl, marijuana, weed, wax, dab, vaping, opioids, cocaine, oxycodone, heroine, nicotine and alcohol, and I loose forth deliverance over them by the blood of Jesus Christ and by the power, anointing, and Spirit of the Living Word of God, in the name of Jesus!

I loose forth the Word of God according to Psalm 107:20, that You sent Your Word to heal them and to deliver them from all destruction.

Thank You for being Jehovah Rapha, their healer and Jehovah Mephalti, their deliverer. I call out their names and command Satan to loose them from their afflictions and addictions and to set them free *now* in the name of Jesus!

For at the name of Jesus, every knee must bow, and every tongue must confess that Jesus Christ is Lord on earth, underneath this earth and in heaven, in the name of Jesus (Philippians 2:10)!

I command their minds to be loosed from the temptation, the appetite from craving the taste, and the ill effects of drug and alcohol use, in the name of Jesus.

If any of my family members are believers who have backslidden, fallen away from the truth, experiencing a crisis of faith or taking Christianity for test drive, I declare Your Word according to 1 Corinthians 10:13, that God who is faithful will not suffer them to be tempted beyond what they are able, but with the temptation, You will make a way of escape, that they may be able to bear it.

I thank You, Father, for loosing them from hanging around people, places, and situations that are not of God and that trigger the use of drugs, alcohol, and any addictive behavior or mindset that is not of God, in the name of Jesus.

I thank You for healing and delivering them from drug and alcohol withdrawals in the name of Jesus!

I thank You for freeing their minds and their bodies from drug and alcohol addictions in the name of Jesus! I thank You for setting them free in the name of Jesus!

I speak healing to the frontal lobe of their brain in the name of Jesus, and I command restoration and a creative miracle of any and every affected area within the frontal lobe of their brain, and I command clear thought patterns in the name of Jesus! I declare in the name of Jesus that they shall have the ability to think rationally, function normally, demonstrate self-control over their emotions to make sound and just decisions, and resist temptation in the name of Jesus. I declare in the name of Jesus that they shall not relapse and instead will live and maintain a sober and godly life in the name of Jesus!

For man looks at the outward appearance, but God looks at the heart (1 Samuel 16:7). Father, in the name of Jesus, I pray that they will confess their sins, repent, and turn back to their first love. Father, You said in 1 John 1:9 that if we confess our sins, You are faithful and just to forgive us of our sins and to cleanse us from all unrighteousness in the name of Jesus.

I bind up any spirit of confusion, self-condemnation, self-rejection, self-hate, guilt, shame, and embarrassment within their minds, and I cast down imaginations and every high thing that exalts itself against the knowledge of God, and I bring every thought into captivity to the obedience of Christ (2 Corinthians 10:5).

Wash them in Your blood and fill them up with the power of Your Holy Spirit. Baptize them with Your Holy Spirit and fire. Anoint their heads with Your oil and fill them up with Your Spirit until it overflows!

As I lift up to You my unsaved loved ones. I declare in the name of Jesus that they shall receive Jesus Christ as their Lord and Savior. I pray in the name of Jesus that their minds will be renewed according to Your Word and that You will send forth divine laborers across their paths to share the Gospel of Jesus Christ.

For Your Word says in Romans 10:9 that if you confess with your mouth Jesus as Lord and believe in your heart that God raised Him from the dead, you will be saved. And according to Romans 10:13, whoever will call on the name of the Lord will be saved. So be it according to Your Word for my loved ones. I declare that they shall confess, believe, and receive the salvation of our Lord and Savior, Jesus Christ.

I declare in the name of Jesus that they will not walk in the counsel of the wicked, or stand in the path of sinners, or sit in the seat of scoffers, but their delight will be in the law of the Lord, and in His law they will meditate day and night, and they will be like a tree firmly planted by the streams of water that yields its fruit in its season, and its leaf does not wither, and in whatever they do, they shall prosper (Psalm 1:1–4).

## Prayer and Declarations for Our Children

I declare that our children shall keep good company in the name of Jesus and that the Word of God will continue to remain hidden in their hearts so that they will not sin against you (1 Corinthians 15:33; Psalm 119:11).

I declare in the name of Jesus that the seed of my womb is blessed and that they are a blessing to others (Deuteronomy 28:4).

Father, You said in your Word, according to Joel 2:28, "It will come about after this That I will pour out My Spirit on all mankind, and your sons and daughters will prophesy, Your old men will dream dreams, Your young men will see visions." So be it unto my children according to Your Word, in Jesus's name.

I declare my blood covenant with You, and I plead the blood of Jesus over my children. I declare the Word of God over my children, and I take a hold of my anointing oil and anoint my children in the name of Jesus (James 5:14; Mark 6:13; Acts 10:38). I declare that my children shall do mighty exploits for Your kingdom, in the name of Jesus. I declare no weapon formed against them shall prosper and that every tongue that rises against them in judgment, they shall condemn in the name of Jesus (Daniel 11:32; Isaiah 54:17)!

I declare that they shall continue a legacy of praise, worship, prayer, and intercession and that they will remain faithful, diligent, and steadfast in the faith.

I declare Isaiah 61:6 in the name of Jesus. My children are priests of the Lord, and they will be spoken of as ministers of our God. They will eat the wealth of nations, and in their riches they will boast.

I declare in the name of Jesus that my children shall have the best education, attend the best colleges and universities, obtain the best jobs and careers, be equally yoked in their marriages, and their future children shall rise up and call them blessed (2 Corinthians 6:14; Proverbs 31:28).

You said in your Word, according to Job 22:28, if we decree a thing, it shall be established unto me, and that the light shall shine upon my ways. So be it as I have decreed these things over and for my children in the name of Lord and my Savior, Jesus Christ.

I declare in the name of Jesus that my children are healed from any and all physical and mental challenges. I declare in the name of Jesus that every one of their needs will be met in the name of Jesus, because You have given us the power and the authority and the faith to call those things that are not as though they were (Romans 4:17).

Therefore, I call those things forth concerning everything that they stand in need of, to be met in the name of Jesus.

For You are Jehovah Jireh (our provider), Jehovah Rehoboth (You open doors), Jehovah Rapha (our healer), and Jehovah Mephalti (our deliver).

## Spiritual Warfare Prayers and Declarations

I bind and rebuke the spirit of fear. For Your Word says that You did not give me the spirit of fear but of power, love, and a sound mind (2 Timothy 1:7).

You have given me the power to tread upon the heads of serpents and scorpions and power over all of the enemy, and nothing shall injure or harm me (Luke 10:19).

Your perfect love casts out all fear, in the name of Jesus (1 John 4:18)! And it is Your love, the love of God, that covers a multitude of sins (1 Peter 4:8)!

With the same love that You have shown toward us, I declare in the name of Jesus that I will demonstrate that love toward my family members, children, friends, coworkers, unsaved loved ones, and those who lead and govern us.

For You said in Your Word, according to 1 John 4:20, "Whoever claims to love God yet hates a brother or sister is a liar. For whoever does not love their brother and sister, whom they have seen, cannot love God, whom they have not seen."

Therefore, I pray in the name of Jesus that I will maintain a spirit of forgiveness in my heart. You said in Your Word to forgive them, for they do not know what they are doing (Luke 23:34). You said in Your Word to forgive our brothers and our sisters seventy times seven (Matthew 18:21–22).

Furthermore, You said in Your Word if you forgive others for their transgressions, your heavenly Father will also forgive you (Matthew 7:10).

As I draw nigh to God, and He will draw nigh to me (James 4:8). Therefore, let me demonstrate Your fruit of the spirit, which is love, joy, peace, patience, kindness, goodness, faithfulness, gentleness, and self-control (Galatians 5:22–23).

Keep my heart, mind, attitude, will, intellect, and emotions in the manner of which You have demonstrated toward us, which is with Your mercy, Your grace, and, above all, Your love, which is the most excellent way (1 Corinthians 12:31).

Love is patient, and love is kind. It does not envy, it does not boast, and it is not proud. It does not dishonor others, it is not self-seeking, it is not easily angered, and it keeps no record of wrongs. Love does not delight in evil but rejoices with the truth. It always protects, always trusts, always hopes, always perseveres. Love never fails (1 Corinthians 13:4–8).

Therefore, I declare that You are perfecting those things that concern me until the day of Christ Jesus (Psalm 138:8). Father, in the name of Jesus, I pray that You will continue to create in me a clean heart and renew a right spirit within me (Psalm 51:10). For God opposes the proud and gives grace to the humble (James 4:6). Help me to represent Your kingdom well and with excellence (Psalm 51:10)!

Your Word says, according to Matthew 24:42-5, to always be ready, because you don't know the day your Lord will come.

I declare in the name of Jesus that I will be confident and have comfort knowing that my redemption draws nigh. Your Word, according to 1 Thessalonians 4:16–17, tells me that the Lord Himself will descend from heaven with a shout, with a voice of the archangel and with the trumpet of God, and the dead in Christ will rise first. Then we who are alive and remain will be caught up together with them in the clouds to meet the Lord in the air, and so we shall always be with the Lord, and therefore we are to comfort one another with these words.

Until You return, I will not be anxious for anything, but in everything by prayer and supplication with thanksgiving I will let my requests be made known to God (Philippians 4:6).

I will take up the full armor of God so that I will be able to resist the evil day, and having done everything to stand, to stand firm. I will stand firm with the belt of truth, the breastplate of righteousness, and having shod my feet with the preparation of the gospel of peace, my shield of faith to extinguish all of the flaming arrows of the evil one, the helmet of salvation, and the sword of the spirit (Ephesians 6:14–17).

I will remain steadfast, immovable, always abounding in the work of the Lord, knowing that my toil is not in vain of the Lord (1 Corinthians 15:58).

I will not grow weary in well doing (Galatians 6:9)! I am strong in the Lord and in the power of His might (Ephesians 6:10)!

Your Holy Spirit strengthens me and sustains me!

I have Your power living inside of me!

I can do all things through Christ who strengthens me (Philippians 4:13), and nothing is impossible for me because I believe (Mark 9:23)!

I thank You, Lord, for doing the impossible in my life. For with God, nothing shall be impossible, and nothing is too hard for God to do (Luke 1:31; Jeremiah 32:37).

I stand in total faith, victory, and confidence, that You, Father God, are the giver of good gifts. You gave Your only begotten Son, Jesus Christ, to die on the cross for my sins. I have full confidence in Your goodness, mercy, grace, and holy Word, that You will come through for me and answer this prayer as it be Your will. In Jesus's name. Amen.

# Personalize Your
## Prayers, Decrees & Declarations

---— DAY ——

# 11

---

## LEADERS
## SPIRITUAL WARFARE
## MY CALLING
## MY PROTECTION

### ADORATION

I magnify Your name! Oh magnify the Lord with me; let us exalt His name together (Psalm 34:3)! For You alone are worthy! For unto us a child is born. Unto us a son is given. And the government will be upon His shoulder. And His name will be called Wonderful, Counselor, Mighty God, Everlasting Father, Prince of Peace (Isaiah 9:6)! I rejoice and bless Your great name because You are the giver of good gifts. You gave me Your only begotten Son, Jesus, to die on the cross for my sins, who died and rose on the third day and got up with all power in His hand, and who appeared to many after the resurrection of His death. You are the living one! The one who lives forevermore and who has the keys of hell and death!

## Confession

Heavenly Father, You said in Your Word, according to 1 John 1:9, if we confess our sins, You are faithful and just to forgive us our sins and to cleanse us from all unrighteousness. God, I'm sorry for falling short in _____ and that my actions in _____ haven't lived up to Your expectations. I repent for not doing_____ when I should have done_____ . Heavenly Father, I let go of all offense, bitterness, anger, and disappointment, and I release it all unto You. I forgive _____, who have hurt me, disappointed me, and caused me any harm. You said in Your Word to forgive other people when they sin against me so that You, heavenly Father, will also forgive me (Matthew 6:14). I receive Your forgiveness. I have no condemnation in Christ (Romans 8:1), and I thank You for helping me to do better the next time. In Jesus's name. Amen.

## Thanksgiving

Hallelujah! I thank You, God, for another day! For this is the day that You have made. I will rejoice and be glad in it (Psalm 118:24). For my times are in your hand, and You are the great I Am (Psalm 31:15). You are the great Jehovah and the lifter of our heads. I thank You for Your mighty acts and Your wonderful works. I rejoice with praise on my lips and thanksgiving in my heart.

For Your Word says in Revelation 1:8, "I am He that liveth, and was dead; and behold, I am alive for evermore, Amen, and have the keys of hell and of death."

I thank You for giving me victory in every area over my life! You always cause me to triumph in the name of Jesus!

I thank You that I am an overcomer in Christ Jesus! I hold fast to faith in Jesus Christ until the end! And this is the victory that overcometh the world, our faith (1 John 5:5)! I have resisted the power and temptation of the enemy and this world system, knowing and trusting in Almighty God for His direction, purpose, and strength to carry out His plans for my life. For Your plans for me are plans not to harm me but to prosper me and give me a future and a hope, in the name of Jesus (Jeremiah 29:11).

## Supplication

### Leaders

I lift up to You my leaders today (names). I pray that they will walk in the spirit, which is pleasing to the Lord.

I pray in the name of Jesus that they will continue to serve the Lord with reverent fear and rejoice with trembling, that they will be willing to obey God's direction and maintain a teachable spirit, in the name of Jesus.

Holy Spirit, I ask that You give them personal direction, teaching, and vision, forever increasing knowledge of God and for revelation of the depths of God and spiritual knowledge of the Word of God.

### Spiritual Warfare

I take action and knock down the barriers and resistance in the spirit in the name of Jesus!

I declare in the name of Jesus that as I humble myself before you and resist the devil on every level with the Word of God, the name of Jesus, and through my blood covenant, the devil must flee in the name of Jesus!

I receive Your Word that I am moving into my promised land, to move to the higher level and your promises in the name of Jesus!

I declare that I am advancing stronger and mightier than ever before. For the kingdom of God suffers violence and the violent (that is men who are eager and with zeal, whose minds are made up, and who care not what force and power they employ to attain the kingdom of heaven, its peace, pardon, and blessedness with as much eagerness as men would snatch and carry off as their own the spoil of a conquered city) take it back by force (like rough and violent bandits seizing their prey, their inheritance, and their purpose to hasten the completion of the kingdom of God and to minister salvation)!

I continue to decree and declare that I am moving into my divine destiny, and I will not be defeated, in the name of Jesus!

For Your plans and purposes for me are good, not to harm me but to prosper me and to give me a future and a hope, in the name of Jesus (Jeremiah 29:11)!

I thank You that my hundredfold return is on the way. I declare in the name of Jesus that a new job is on the way, promotion is on the way, a new place to stay is on the way, new homes are on the way. Food, clothing, and everything I stand in need of is on the way. I thank you that prison gates and doors of opportunity are being opened for our loved ones. I decree and declare in the name of Jesus that our loved ones are being loosed, let go, and set free.

I decree and declare in the name of Jesus that God's mercy and grace are being granted toward them, a spirit of forgiveness and favor is being released in the courtrooms, unjust charges are being overturned, and the King's heart is being turned toward our loved ones. They are being loosed, let go, and set free in the name of Jesus! I thank You that divine doors are opening up for them now, in Jesus's name!

For you are Jehovah Rehoboth. You open doors for us. You are Lord, and You have given us room, and we will flourish in the land (Genesis 26:22).

Thank You, Jesus, that You are He who opens, and no man can shut. Thank You, Jesus, that you are He who shuts, and no man opens (Revelation 3:7).

I declare in the name of Jesus that doors are opening by the power of Your Spirit. For where the Spirit of the Lord is, there is liberty, there is freedom. I thank You for open doors of freedom, and I bind the spirit of demonic oppression that would keep me or my loved ones from experiencing Your goodness and freedom to live an abundant life.

You came to give us life and life abundantly.

I shall see the goodness of the Lord in the land of the living.

With long life, you shall satisfy me and show us Your salvation (Psalm 91:16).

For You said in Your Word that You shall supply all of my needs according to Your riches in glory in Christ Jesus (Philippians 4:19).

And it is You, Lord, who gives me the ability to produce wealth, and so confirms his covenant, which he swore to our ancestors, as it is today, in the name of Jesus (Philippians 4:19; Deuteronomy 8:18)!

You said in Your Word, according to Ecclesiastes 5:19, it is a good thing to receive wealth from God and the good health to enjoy it. To enjoy your work and accept your lot in life—this is indeed a gift from God.

I declare in the name of Jesus that above all things, I shall prosper and be in good health, even as my soul prospers in the name of Jesus (3 John 1:2)!

I declare in the name of Jesus that sickness and disease cannot stay in my body. I speak to my body and declare that my body is the temple of the Holy Spirit and I am the healed and not the sick.

For You are Jehovah Rapha, the Lord God who heals.

I declare in the name of Jesus that I will not be cheated out of my destiny and out of every dream and vision that You have placed on my heart and have called me to do in the name of Jesus!

I declare Your Word, that You came to give me life and life more abundantly in the name of Jesus (John 10:10)!

Therefore, I will not be moved by what I hear, feel, and see, only by the Word of God!

I will not accept any manipulation or negative words spoken over me, to me, or over my children, or to my children, or my grandchildren, my marriage, my relationship, my ministry, and my businesses in the name of Jesus. I declare that my seed is blessed in the name of Jesus!

Father, in the name of Jesus, help me to appropriate an RIR principle to renounce, interrupt, and resist. I declare in the name of Jesus that I will renounce evil words spoken to me, over me, and everything concerning me and everyone and everything that pertains to me quickly, in the name of Jesus. I declare in the name of Jesus that I will interrupt ungodly and negative thought patterns quickly, in the name of Jesus! I will resist the lies and the accusations of the devil in the name of Jesus!

I declare in the name of Jesus that I will not allow Satan or his imps or people to try to keep me in a realm that they think I should stay in, in the name of Jesus!

For I am the head and not the tail, and I am above and not beneath (Deuteronomy 28:13)! The last shall be first, and the first shall be last (Matthew 20:16)!

This is my season and my set time for favor, and I declare in the name of Jesus that I am walking into and/or through 2022 and beyond (name your year) with the fullness of God's supernatural blessings concerning every aspect of my life, according to His Word and with His favor, His anointing, and the power of His Holy Spirit! I declare in the name of Jesus that I am an example of God's total prosperity!

For I wrestle not against flesh and blood (Ephesians 6:12)!

The devil is a liar, the father of lies, the accuser of the brethren, the prince of the air, and I shut him down with the Word of God in the name of Jesus!

I keep the enemy under my feet in the name of Jesus, with the Word of God, the armor of God, the power of God, the anointing of God, the name of Jesus, and my blood-bought covenant with my Lord and Savior, Jesus Christ!

## My Calling

I declare in the name of Jesus that God is breaking through glass ceilings for me and is causing me to break forth into my destiny!

I declare in the name of Jesus that I will do everything that the Lord has called me to do!

For who the Lord has called, He has equipped; who the Lord has called, He has predestined; and those He predestined, He also called; those He called, He also justified; those He justified, He also glorified (Romans 8:30; Hebrews 13:20–21).

What then shall we say in response to these things? If God is for us, who can be against us (Romans 8:31)?

Therefore, there is nothing that the devil can do about it, in Jesus's name!

## My Protection

Father, in the name of Jesus, You said in Your Word, "Touch not my anointed and do my prophet no harm" (Psalm 105:15)! Therefore, I declare Psalm 91:1–16, Your holy, written Word for my protection:

> He who dwells in the shelter of the Most High Will abide in the shadow of the Almighty. I will say to the LORD, "My refuge and my fortress, My God, in whom I trust!" For it is He who delivers you from the snare of the trapper and from the deadly pestilence. He will cover you with His pinions and under His wings you may seek refuge; His faithfulness is a shield and bulwark. You will not be afraid of the terror by night, or of the arrow that flies by day; Of the pestilence that stalks in darkness, or of the destruction that lays waste at noon. A thousand may fall at your side and ten thousand at your right hand, but it shall not approach you. You will only look on with your eye and see the recompense of the wicked. For you have made the LORD, my refuge, even the Most High, your dwelling place. No evil will befall you, Nor will any plague come near your tent. For He will give His angels charge concerning you, to guard you in all your ways. They will bear you up in their hands, that you do not strike your foot against a stone. You will tread upon the lion

and cobra, the young lion and the serpent you will trample down. Because he has loved Me, therefore I will deliver him; I will set him securely on high, because he has known My name. He will call upon Me, and I will answer him; I will be with him in trouble; I will rescue him and honor him. With a long life I will satisfy him And let him see My salvation.

Thank You, heavenly Father, for not letting my foot slip (Psalm 121:3)!

Thank You, Lord, for upholding me with Your righteous right hand. My times are in Your hands (Isaiah 41:10; Psalm 31:15)!

I declare in the name of Jesus my righteousness shall go before me, and the Lord's glory shall be my rear guard (Isaiah 58:8).

I declare in the name of Jesus no weapon formed against me shall prosper, and every tongue that rises up against me in judgment, I shall condemn (Isaiah 54:17)!

So shall they fear the name of the Lord from the west, and His glory from the rising of the sun.

When the enemy shall come in like a flood, the Spirit of the Lord shall lift up a standard against him (Isaiah 59:19).

I'm enlarging the place of my tent, and I am stretching my tent curtains wide! I will not hold back. I will lengthen my cords and will strengthen my stakes (Isaiah 54:2)!

I'm going forth, and I'm going to be about my Father's business in the name of Jesus. I declare in the name of Jesus that I'm covered by the blood of Jesus and with the anointing and the power of the Holy Ghost in Jesus's name!

I am unmovable, unstoppable, and undefeated in the name of Jesus!

I am not confined by what I cannot do and where I cannot go because I have a lot of things to speak forth, decree, and declare—and that is the infallible Word of the Living God!

As I decree a thing, it shall be established unto me in the name of Jesus (Job 22:28)!

I do not have any doubt in my heart concerning the Word of God and the promises of God. I believe by faith in God's Word and according to God's Word, that I shall have what I say, in the name of Jesus (Mark 11:23–24).

I shall have a promotion in the natural and spiritual realm. I shall have a new life, a new job, a new career, a new home, a new house, a new business, a new ministry, a new bank account full of money, a new car, a new heart, a new mind, a new church, a new building—for behold, Jesus makes all things new (Revelation 21:5)!

"See, I AM doing a new thing! Now it springs up; do you not perceive it? I AM making a way in the wilderness and streams in the wasteland" (Isaiah 43:19).

I declare in the name of Jesus the I Am that I Am is causing me to prosper, my children to prosper, my children's children to prosper, my family to prosper, my marriage to prosper, my relationships to prosper, my ministry to prosper, my finances to prosper and my _____ to prosper in the name of Jesus!

As I humble myself before You, Lord, with fasting, prayer, intercession, decrees, and declarations, I praise You and I bless Your holy name. For You are the one who exalts me. It is You who makes us a great nation, and it is You who blesses us. And it is You who makes me famous (make my name great), so that I will be a blessing to others (Genesis 12:2).

I thank You for your promises, that You will bless those who bless me, and the ones who curse me, you will curse (Genesis 12:3).

Hallelujah! I am the seed of Abraham, and because I am the seed of Abraham, I receive my inheritance, and I am blessed!

I bless Your great name that Your promise still stands to this day!

You are a God who does not change. Thank You, Jesus, for You are the same yesterday, today, and forever (Hebrews 13:8)!

Heaven and earth shall pass away, but Your Word will never pass away! Your Word does not return unto You void! But it shall accomplish that which You please, and it shall prosper in the manner of which You sent it (Isaiah 55:11)!

Oh how great is Your faithfulness!

Thank You for making my name great. Thank You, oh God, for making me famous. Thank You, Almighty God, for making me into a great nation. I thank You, all-sufficient one, for showering down blessings upon me in order to be able to shower down blessings upon others (Genesis 12:2; Psalm 45:17). I am blessed and highly favored. I will be unapologetic about it, in the name of Jesus.

I shall see the goodness of the Lord in the land of the living (Psalm 27:13)!

You came to give me life and life more abundantly (John 10:10).

I declare that I will stay ready until my redemption draws nigh, and as I stay ready, I will continue to occupy until You come in the name of Jesus.

You, God Almighty alone, will get all of the glory, all of the honor, and all of the praise!

All praise, all honor, and all glory belong to You and only You, heavenly Father!

I decree and declare in the name of Jesus that I shall walk in Your glory and rest in Your glory! I will walk day by day with the praises of the Most High God on my lips and in my heart!

I walk in total humility and submission unto You, and I honor You from my heart every morning by giving You my first fruits of prayer, intercession, decrees, and declarations. Thank You for the manifestation of this prayer. In Jesus's name. Amen.

# Personalize Your
## Prayers, Decrees & Declarations

# 12

## EARTHLY LEADERS
## SPIRITUAL LEADERS
## SALVATION

### ADORATION

Oh sing unto the Lord a new song; sing all the earth. Sing unto the Lord. Bless His name. Proclaim good tidings of His salvation from day to day. Tell of His glory among the nations, His wonderful deeds among the peoples. For great is the Lord and greatly to be praised (Psalm 96:1)!

### CONFESSION

Heavenly Father, You said in Your Word, according to 1 John 1:9, if we confess our sins, You are faithful and just to forgive us our sins and to cleanse us from all unrighteousness. God, I'm sorry for falling short in _____ and that my actions in _____ haven't lived up to Your expectations. I repent for not doing_____ when I should have done_____ . Heavenly Father, I let go of all offense, bitterness, anger, and disappointment, and I release it all unto You. I forgive _____, who have hurt me, disappointed me, and caused me any harm. You said in Your Word to forgive other people when they sin against me so that You, heavenly Father, will also forgive me (Matthew 6:14). I receive Your forgiveness. I have no condemnation in Christ (Romans 8:1), and I thank You for helping me to do better the next time. In Jesus's name. Amen.

## Thanksgiving

I thank You, and I praise You. I will bless the Lord at all times, and His praise shall continually be in my mouth (Psalm 34:1)! I thank You, Jehovah Mekaddishkem, for sanctifying me and setting me apart. I thank You, heavenly Father, for anointing me with power and Your Holy Spirit.

Have Your way, Holy Spirit, in me; use me as Your vessel to edify, exhort, and comfort others through prayer and intercession. Your Word says the effectual, fervent prayer of a righteous man availeth much (James 5:16).

With all prayer and petition, I will continue to pray at all times in the Spirit, and with this in view, I will be on the alert with all perseverance and petition for all the saints (Ephesians 6:18).

## Supplication

## Earthly Leaders

I lift up to You our earthly leaders, those who govern over us from the federal, state, and local levels.

I declare a hedge of protection around them and their families. Lord, I ask that You help them in the areas where they need help. For Your Word says that You are our very present help in the time of trouble (Psalm 46:1).

I also pray that You will continue to help them make the right decisions concerning the affairs of this country, as it pertains to our health, safety, protection, and well-being.

I thank You in advance for sending forth divine laborers across their path to witness to them if they are not saved, if they are lost, or if they have fallen away from the faith, in order to receive salvation.

## Spiritual Leaders

I lift up to You my spiritual leaders today (name them).

I declare Psalm 91:10, 11, that no evil shall befall them, nor will any plague come near their dwelling. For He will give His angels charge concerning them and guard them in all of their ways.

I declare divine health for our leaders spiritually, mentally and emotionally, in the name of Jesus. I command all effects of tiredness and any form of discouragement to be loosed from their bodies and minds in the name of Jesus!

I declare that their youth is being renewed like an eagle and that above all things, they shall prosper and be in good health as their souls prosper in the name of Jesus (Psalm 103:5; 3 John 1:2)!

I also declare that they shall have adequate strength to accomplish every task that is set before them in the name of Jesus!

I declare in the name of Jesus that they are strong in You and in the power of Your might (Ephesians 6:10). I declare in the name of Jesus that is in You that they live, move, and have their being (Acts 17:28). I declare, as their days go, so shall their strength be (Deuteronomy 33:25)!

## Salvation

And while keeping myself in the love of God, waiting anxiously for the mercy of our Lord Jesus Christ to eternal life, I shall seek to save others, snatching them out of the fire in the name of Jesus (Jude 1:23).

I declare a harvest of souls and lives will be changed in the name of Jesus!

You know of Jesus of Nazareth, how God anointed Him with the Holy Spirit and with power and how he went about doing good, healing all who were oppressed by the devil, for God was with Him (Acts 10:38).

So be it unto me as I go forward full of faith and in the Holy Spirit and with the anointing and power of God, in the name of Jesus.

All glory, honor, and praise belongs unto You. Thank You, heavenly Father, for using me to be Your representative on this earth to be a great witness for You, to help save the lost and to be a blessing to others. Thank You, Lord, for fulfilling every promise You have spoken to me according to Your Word and within this prayer. In Jesus's name. Amen.

# Personalize Your
## Prayers, Decrees & Declarations

EARTHLY LEADERS

SPIRITUAL WARFARE

FOR THOSE WHO ARE STRUGGLING

FOR THOSE EXPERIENCING
FINANCIAL HARDSHIP

SALVATION

HEALING AND DELIVERANCE

## ADORATION

Father, in the name of Jesus, I come before You this day to tell You that I love You, adore You, and appreciate You. I love You with all of my heart, all of my soul, and with all of my might (Deuteronomy 6:5). You are the great Jehovah. For the Lord God is the great God, the great king above all gods (Psalm 95:3)!

## CONFESSION

Heavenly Father, You said in Your Word, according to 1 John 1:9, if we confess our sins, You are faithful and just to forgive us our sins and to cleanse

us from all unrighteousness. God, I'm sorry for falling short in _____
and that my actions in _____ haven't lived up to Your expectations. I
repent for not doing_____ when I should have done_____
. Heavenly Father, I let go of all offense, bitterness, anger, and disappointment,
and I release it all unto You. I forgive _____, who have hurt
me, disappointed me, and caused me any harm. You said in Your Word to
forgive other people when they sin against me so that You, heavenly Father,
will also forgive me (Matthew 6:14). I receive Your forgiveness. I have no
condemnation in Christ (Romans 8:1), and I thank You for helping me to do
better the next time. In Jesus's name. Amen.

## THANKSGIVING

I thank You for Your unfailing love and that You continue to show Yourself
strong through me concerning Your promises. For Your promises to me
are always yes and amen (2 Corinthians 1:20). I thank You, God, for Your
presence, your Holy Spirit, Your power and peace. I thank You, God, for Your
anointing. It's the anointing that destroys every yoke and sets the captives free.
I thank You that You hear me every time I pray, that Your eyes are on the
righteous, and Your ears are attentive to my cry (Psalm 34:15).

## SUPPLICATION

## EARTHLY LEADERS

Father, in the name of Jesus, I lift up to You our earthly leaders, the president
and his/her family and his/her cabinet and their families, the vice president
and his/her family, the president's cabinet and their families, the Senate, and
all those who govern over us at the federal, state, and local levels.

I plead the blood of Jesus over them, and I declare a hedge of protection
around them in the name of Jesus.

I thank You for protecting them from danger seen and unseen, evil seen
and unseen, and that they will not be distracted or deterred by Satan's devices.

I declare in the name of Jesus that You will give our earthly leaders and
those who govern over us wisdom and direction to make sound and just

decisions and to stay alert concerning the protection, safety, and well-being of this country and of all people who dwell in it.

I thank You for sending forth divine laborers across their path to witness to them if they are not saved or are lost. I pray in the name of Jesus that they shall receive the gift of salvation and will be endowed by Your Holy Spirit to help advance the kingdom of God.

During this season, I plead the blood of Jesus over myself, my children, my family, my place of employment, the market places, the routes I travel, every financial institution, every nonprofit and government entity, our school systems, economic systems, health systems, departments of corrections, and all lines of international, domestic, and foreign trade and communication.

I declare the divine safety, peace, protection, and intervention concerning every citizen in this country and across the world in the name of Jesus.

I take authority and declare that no weapon formed against the body of Christ and the United States of America shall prosper, and every tongue that rises against us in judgment, we shall condemn in the name of Jesus (Isaiah 54:17). I declare that the gates of hell will not prevail against us, in the name of Jesus (Matthew 16:18)!

I bind and rebuke the spirits of deception and fear in the name of Jesus.

I will not be ignorant of the enemies' devices, and I declare that America will not be ignorant of the devil's devices (2 Corinthians 2:11).

I decree and declare that America will not respond in fear.

I decree and declare that America is great not because of the world or man's agenda or because of specific movements but because America was already predestined by Elohim, our Creator, to be one nation under God, indivisible, with liberty and justice for all!

I decree and declare that America and those who govern America will respond in truth, unity, power, prayer, peace, love, and justice through the superiority, rule, reign, jurisdiction, and the powers that be, which is Almighty God, the I Am that I Am, in the name of Jesus.

I thank You that Your angels are taking charge concerning America and are guarding us in all of our ways (Psalm 91:11)!

I thank You, heavenly Father, that as we come together in unity and love and on one accord in Your name, that one will put a thousand to flight, and two will put ten thousand to flight, according to Your Word (Deuteronomy 32:30)!

I thank You that iron is sharpening iron as one man sharpens another (Proverbs 27:17). Hallelujah to Your great name! I thank You for the outpouring of Your Holy Spirit among our church (name your church) and every church in America and across all nations. I pray for Your Holy Spirit to rest and dwell upon all intercessors to keep watch, travail in the spirit, groan, weep, wail, and pray victorious prayers—chain-breaking prayers and yoke-destroying prayers, with the anointing and the Word of God over America! I decree and declare that we will not break rank until we see the changes that God wants to see and make the change that God wants to make in the name of Jesus!

## Spiritual Warfare

I thank You for the anointing of God and that the atmosphere of heaven is upon us and our church as we come together in unity.

I declare Isaiah 61:1–3, "The Spirit of Lord God is upon us, because the Lord has anointed us to bring good news to the afflicted. You have sent us to bind up the brokenhearted, to proclaim liberty to the captives and freedom to the prisoners. To proclaim the favorable year of the Lord and the vengeance of our God. To comfort all who mourn. To grant those who mourn in Zion, giving them a garland instead of ashes, the oil of gladness instead of a spirit of fainting, and the planting of the Lord that He may be glorified!"

I thank You, Lord, for giving me the power and authority to bind and to loose. For whatever I bind on earth is bound in heaven, and whatever I loose on earth will be loosed in heaven (Matthew 18:18).

Therefore, I bind up the spirit of unforgiveness, rejection, hatred, bitterness, resentment, and offensiveness, and I loose forth the love of God and the peace of God in the name of Jesus.

For the love of God covers a multitude of sins, and I declare the peace of God that surpasses all understanding shall guard our hearts and our minds in Christ Jesus (1 Peter 4:8; Philippians 4:7).

I bind up and arrest the forces of darkness and the spirits of fear, hate, anger, rage, terroristic attacks, murder, strife, prejudice, racism, discord, chaos, division, and mayhem in the jurisdiction that you have given me authority over in the name of Jesus Christ.

I take authority in the name of Jesus Christ, and I loose forth the Word of God, which is quick, powerful, and sharper than any two-edged sword, piercing even to the dividing asunder of soul and spirit and of the joints and marrow, and is a discerner of the thoughts and intents of the heart (Hebrews 4:12).

For this purpose the Son of God was manifested, that He might destroy the works of the devil (1 John 3:8). I declare and decree that the works of the devil are destroyed over my life, over my goals and dreams, over my children and family, over my marriage, over this nation and country, and over my job, finances, ministry, business, and relationships in the name of Jesus.

Jesus Christ spoiled all principalities and powers and made a public spectacle of them by triumphing over them on the cross (Colossians 2:15).

I declare, in the name of Jesus, I will not be moved by what I see, hear, or feel. I pray from a position of dominion and authority, victory and defeat over the enemy, and I take a hold of my dominion and authority, and I pray!

I will pray without ceasing (1 Thessalonians 5:16). I will pray in my most holy faith (Jude 1:20)!

Hallelujah, I praise Your holy name, Jesus!

I will persevere in the faith, war in the spirit, resist the enemy, and refute and interrupt every lie and scheme of the devil and his imps. I will renounce every unproductive and negative thought and voice of the enemy. I will fight the good fight of faith, and I will be strong and courageous in the Lord, and I will win in the name of Jesus (1 Timothy 6:12; Joshua 1:9)!

I declare and decree that I always win, and I always triumph in the name of Jesus (1 Corinthians 15:57)!

I declare that no evil shall befall me, and no plague shall come near my dwelling in the name of Jesus (Psalm 91:10)!

I thank You for giving me power to tread on serpents and scorpions and over all the power of the enemy (Luke 10:19).

I thank You that I am moving forward and taking ground with a double-edged sword in my mouth to defeat my giants.

For You are Adoni, my Lord and master! You are Jehovah Mephalti, my deliverer! I thank You for being the only true and Living God, who shuts the mouths of lions (Daniel 6:22).

When the enemy comes in like a flood, the spirit of the Lord will lift up a standard, Jehovah Nissi, the Lord, my banner and my protector (Isaiah 59:19). I declare in the name of Jesus the Lord is fighting for me, putting the enemy to flight, and moving the enemy out of the midst of my circumstances.

I thank You that the weapons of my warfare are not carnal but are mighty through God to the pulling down of strongholds (2 Corinthians 10:4).

I thank You that the Word of God, my prayers, praise, and worship are bombarding the heavens like a sweet-smelling fragrance into Your nostrils (Revelation 8:3). Let the Word of God and every prayer, decree, declaration, and petition fill the earth with Your glory, manifest Your presence, and cause Your hand to supernaturally move in our favor.

I thank You, Father, that no matter what it looks like, what I hear, how I feel, or what I see, You are causing everything to work together for my good because I love You and am called according to Your purpose (Romans 8:28). I thank You, Father, that everything that the enemy meant for evil You are turning around for my good (Genesis 50:20).

I thank You and trust You. I bless Your holy name because You are a faithful God! You told me in Your Word that those who trust in the Lord will not be made ashamed (Psalm 23:3).

Your integrity can never be compromised! You are faithful to do what you have promised (Hebrews 10:23)!

For God is not a man, that he should lie, neither the son of man, that he should repent (Numbers 23:19).

I thank You, Father God, for being mindful of me and that You hasten to Your Word to perform it (Jerimiah 1:12; Psalm 115:12).

## FOR THOSE WHO ARE STRUGGLING

Father, in the name of Jesus, I lift up to You the people today who are struggling and are in need of Your mercy and grace.

Just as God instructed Zerubbabel to speak grace to the mountain, the mountain being the hindrance of Satan, who opposed anyone trying to rebuild the temple, I speak the grace of God to every situation and circumstance that people are going through. The Lord said, "Who are you, O great mountain? Before Zerubbable you shall become a plain! And he shall bring forth the capstone with shouts of Grace, grace to it" (Zechariah 4:7).

God, You are all-powerful, sovereign, and full of mercy and grace. I pray in the name of Jesus that you turn things around for the better for all humankind and those who are in times of distress.

I shout grace to sickness, disease, poverty, lack, debt, fear, disappointment, setbacks, resistance, and delays, and I command those mountains to be utterly destroyed and brought down to naught in the name of Jesus.

I invite Your Holy Spirit to work a miracle in every situation and circumstance people are facing. I speak grace to every immovable mountain the enemy puts in front of them. For the enemy can never stand against what God desires to do by His grace.

I declare by faith that they will have the strength and courage to persevere through all situations and circumstances, even through opposition.

For those who are saved and are going through various circumstances in their lives, I pray in the name of Jesus that You encourage their hearts. Your Word says the just shall live by faith (Romans 1:17). I pray they will stand strong in their faith in God because faith is the substance of all things hoped for, the evidence of things not seen (Hebrews 11:1).

God said in His Word that if we have faith the size of a mustard seed, we can say to the mountain, "Be thou removed and cast into the sea and do not doubt in our heart, but believe that those things he says will be done, he will have whatever he says" (Matthew 17:20).

For without faith, it is impossible to please Him, for he who comes to God must believe that He is and that He is a rewarder of those who diligently seek Him (Hebrews 11:6).

I am fully convinced that You, heavenly Father, will do as all You promised to do according to Your Word.

I trust You, God, that You are able to do exceedingly and abundantly above all that I can ask, think, or imagine (Ephesians 3:20).

For there is nothing too hard for You to do (Jeremiah 32:27).

With You, God, all things are possible (Matthew 19:26). My trust in You is unwavering. You are my commander in chief. No one serving as a soldier gets entangled in civilian affairs but rather tries to please his commanding officer (2 Timothy 2:4).

Therefore, I trust You without a doubt, and I obey You without a question because I have strong faith. I believe that You are the great I Am that I Am. You are the great Jehovah, God Almighty, Elohim, the Creator of heaven and earth. My faith in You, heavenly Father, is a weapon. It is my shield, a part of my holy armor that destroys and quenches every fiery dart and the work of the enemy.

No matter what's happening in and around me, my faith in You and Your holy Word is my response and a weapon against the enemy.

Because I have faith in You and trust You, I will not be made ashamed (Romans 10:11; Psalm 25:3). You are faithful to Your Word to perform it. You hasten to Your Word to perform it (Jeremiah 1:12).

I set my mind to dwell on the ability of God to do the impossible. For with God, nothing shall be impossible (Luke 1:37).

## For Those Experiencing Financial Hardship

I lift up to You those who are experiencing financial hardship. I declare that You are Jehovah Jireh, that You are a God who looks ahead and makes provision for them.

Father, in the name of Jesus, You said in Your Word that You are the Lord God that supplies all of our needs according to Your riches in glory, in Christ Jesus (Philippians 4:19).

I pray in the name of Jesus for a divine, supernatural, financial miracle to take place in their lives (Psalm 77:14; 1)!

I pray in the name of Jesus that they may be blessed by the Lord, the maker of heaven and earth. The highest heavens belong to the Lord, but the earth He has given to humankind (Psalm 115:15–16).

I declare that Your divine power, Lord, has given them all things that pertain to life and godliness, through the knowledge of he who has called us to glory and virtue (2 Peter 1:3).

Both riches and honor come from You, and You are the ruler over all. In Your hands are power and might to exalt and give strength to all (1 Chronicles 29:12).

I thank You for opening up doors for them that no man can shut (Revelation 3:7).

I decree and declare in the name of Jesus new employment, new jobs, promotions, and extraordinary and unexpected supernatural favor.

I thank You for breaking through glass ceilings for them. I declare in the name of Jesus that You are fighting for them and moving our enemies out of their way. I thank You, heavenly Father, for preparing a table before them in the presence of their enemies and that You anoint their heads with oil until it overflows (Psalm 23:5).

For David went to Baal Perazim, and there he defeated the Philistines, and David said, "The Lord has broken through my enemies like a flood." For you are the Lord of the breakthrough (2 Samuel 5:20). Thank You for breaking through for them.

I declare that You are creating new streams of revenue for them and that You are causing them to prosper in the name of Jesus. I thank You for increasing their finances so that they are able to provide for their children and families in the name of Jesus.

I declare in the name of Jesus that You are causing others to shower down blessings on them so that they will be able to shower down blessings on others.

I thank You for making provision and paying every bill that needs to be paid, rent that needs to be paid, car notes that need to be paid, mortgages that need to be paid, tuition that needs to be paid, and providing healthy and satisfying food on their table in the name of Jesus.

I thank You that I serve the great I Am and that You can do the impossible for them.

I declare in the name of Jesus that Your people will be financially free and stable, nothing missing, lacking, or broken. I decree and declare that wealth and riches will be in their households (Psalm 112:3).

I thank You, and I praise Your great name! I declare that they shall see the goodness of the Lord in the land of the living (Psalm 27:13).

For You are the Lord God, who supplies all of their needs according to your riches in glory, in Christ Jesus (Philippians 4:19).

I declare in the name of Jesus that You are opening up doors for them that no man can shut and that their gifts are making room for them and bringing them before great men (Revelation 3:7; Proverbs 18:16).

I thank You, Father, that You are causing Your face to shine upon them and that You encamp around them as a shield of favor (Numbers 6:24–26; Psalm 5:12).

I thank You, Father, that You did not give them the spirit of fear but of power and love and a sound mind (1 Timothy 1:7).

I thank You for loosing and setting Your people free from anxiety, fear, depression, schizophrenia, every mental illness, every physical and medical complication, and drug and alcohol addictions in the name of Jesus.


## DELIVERANCE OF LEVIATHAN AND MARINE SPIRITS

Father, in the name of Jesus Christ of Nazareth, I come before You to seek healing, deliverance, mercy, and grace. For You are Jehovah Rapha, our healer, the Lord God, and you are Jehovah Mephalti, the Lord God that delivers.

I thank You that Your Word says that we can come boldly to Your throne of grace to obtain mercy in the time of need (Hebrews 4:16).

For You are the same yesterday and today and forever (Hebrews 13:8).

I come before You humbly. I ask that You forgive my sins of omission and commission, things I have said and done knowingly and unknowingly.

I repent of any and all sin that has caused the enemy to gain a foothold in my life.

I renounce and we repent of sexual sins, promiscuity, juvenile delinquency, prostitution, sexual immorality, seducing spirits, sorceries, enchantments, divination, freemasonry involvement and activity, any involvement and practices of black magic, witchcraft, idolatry, antichrist, self-worship, false religion, ungodly marriages, disobedience, pride, doubt, deception, rebellion, control, persecuting others, caging of souls, seeking false spirit guides, hatred, murder, bloodshed, greed, abortions, death, infidelity, succumbing to a poverty mindset, exercising a lack of self-control, and bitterness. I renounce these sins and of my bloodline, back four and twenty-five generations in the name of Jesus.

I plead the blood of Jesus over myself, my family, and my generational bloodline back four and twenty-five generations fold. I decree and declare in Jesus's name that this day forward, my bloodline is blessed, healed, delivered, and free from sin and the bondage of the enemy. The blood of Jesus Christ has redeemed me and my family from the curse of the law.

I decree and declare in the name of Jesus that You have given me the keys of the kingdom (power and authority) and the authority to bind and loose. For whatever I bind in heaven is bound on earth, and whatever I loose on earth will be loosed in heaven (Matthew 16:19; Matthew 18:18).

In the name of Jesus Christ of Nazareth, I bind up the water spirit of Mami Wata, which is the transcultural pantheon of water spirits and ditties of the African diaspora.

In the name of Jesus Christ of Nazareth, I bind up the Owu Mmiri spirit, which is the mermaid-like spirit of water from the riverine people of Nigeria.

I bind up the Kappa, and the Kawataro water spirit known as the river child, and the Hyosube water spirit, which is of the like, in the name of Jesus.

I bind up the leviathan and marine spirits in the name of Jesus.

I break the heads of leviathan that seek to embellish pride and to cause chaos, confusion, strife, and unrest in the name of Jesus (Psalm 74:14; Psalm 104:25–26; James 3:16).

I thank You, God, for smashing the heads of the dragons in the sea (Psalm 74:13).

Let the waters of the deep be dried up and destroy every spirit of leviathan in the name of Jesus (Job 41:31; Isaiah 44:27).

I call forth a drought upon leviathan's waters in the name of Jesus (Jeremiah 50:38; Jeremiah 51:36).

In the name of Jesus Christ of Nazareth, I decree and declare that the waters of leviathan's river will dry up, and the riverbed will be parched and dry (Isaiah 19:5).

I break all curses of pride and leviathan from my life in the name of Jesus.

In the name of Jesus Christ of Nazareth, I draw out leviathan with a fishhook, and I press down his tongue with a cord. I put a rope in his nose and pierce his jaw with a hook (Job 41:1–2).

I decree and declare in the name of Jesus that no evil or proud waters will flow from my life (Psalm 124:5).

I decree and declare that the channels of the waters are seen at Your rebuke, Lord, in the name of Jesus (Psalm 18:15).

I call down fire from heaven to burn up every demonic spirit associated with marine spirits and leviathan, in the name of Jesus Christ of Nazareth.

Father God, bring down the proud demons that have exalted themselves against Your people.

Father, in the name of Jesus, I rebuke and destroy every trap the devil has set for me. I decree and declare that plans of the enemy will not prosper but be exposed (Psalm 140:5).

Therefore, I bind up and cast out all mind control and manipulative spirits of the octopus and squid in the name of Jesus Christ of Nazareth.

I thank You, heavenly Father, for deliverance. You sent Your Word to heal me and to deliver me from all destruction (Psalm 107:20).

For this reason, You summoned the twelve and began to send them out in pairs and gave them authority over the unclean spirits, to cast out many demons and to anoint with oil many sick people and to heal them in the name of Jesus (Mark 6:7, 13).

I thank You, Jesus, that as Your discipline, You have given me authority and power to overcome all of the power of the enemy (Luke 10:19).

I thank You, God, for being my deliverer!

Thank you for making haste to deliver me (Psalm 70:1).

Thank You, God, for delivering me from the power of the wicked, from the clutches of cruel oppressors (Psalm 71:4).

Thank You, God, for delivering me out of great waters in the name of Jesus (Psalm 144:7).

Thank You, God, for delivering me out of my distress in the name of Jesus (Psalm 107:6).

Thank You, God, for delivering my soul from death, my eyes from tears, and my feet from falling in the name of Jesus (Psalm 116:8).

I will stand in faith and continue to command deliverance for my life in the name of Jesus (Psalm 44:4).

I thank You, God, for delivering me from all fear in the name of Jesus. For you did not give me a spirit of fear but of power and love and a sound mind, in Jesus's name (Psalm 34:4; 2 Timothy 1:7).

I decree and declare in the name of Jesus that as I call upon the name of the Lord Jesus Christ, I am delivered (Joel 2:32).

For in the presence of the Lord, there is liberty and freedom. I thank You for freedom from the hands of the enemy in the name of Jesus.

For whom the Son sets free is free indeed (2 Corinthians 3:17).

And it shall come to pass in that day that his burden shall be taken away from off thy shoulder, and his yoke from off thy neck, and the yoke shall be destroyed because of the anointing. I thank You, Almighty God. I receive the anointing of God that destroys every yoke and sets the captives free (Isaiah 10:27).

I receive the miracles of deliverance in my life. In Jesus's name. Amen (Daniel 6:27).


## HEALING AND DELIVERANCE

I thank You for a hedge of protection and covering over those who are in prison, who are homeless on the street, families living in their cars, those who are struggling, single mothers with children, single fathers with children, those who are divorced or going through a divorce, the widows and orphans, and for children and families in abusive situations.

I thank You for delivering them out of their situations in the name of Jesus.

I plead the blood of Jesus over them and declare Your divine safety and protection for them and that your angels are taking charge concerning them and are guarding them in all of their ways, in the name of Jesus (Psalm 91:11).

I thank You for being their very present help in the time of trouble in the name of Jesus (Psalm 46:1).

I thank You for being their refuge, their hope, and making a way of escape for them in the name of Jesus (1 Corinthians 10:13).

I bind up the spirit of fear, anxiety, and depression in the name of Jesus, and I loose forth the Word of God.

I declare in the name of Jesus that You did not give them the spirit of fear but of power, love, and a sound mind (1 Timothy 1:7).

I declare in the name of Jesus that they will not fear the terror of night, or the arrow that flies by day, or the pestilence that stalks in the darkness, or the plague that destroys at midday (Psalm 91:6).

I declare in the name of Jesus they will be anxious for nothing, but in every situation, by prayer and petition, with thanksgiving, they will present their requests to God. And the peace of God that surpasses all understanding shall guard their hearts and minds in Christ Jesus (Philippians 4:6–7).

Let God arise and their enemies be scattered in the name of Jesus (Psalm 68:1)!

I cast out the spirit of depression and every symptom of depression that includes insomnia, a lack of appetite, the inability to concentrate, low self-esteem, lack of engagement in pleasurable activities, suicidal ideation, recurrent suicidal ideation and attempts in the name of Jesus. I command the spirit of depression and all of its symptoms to flee from Your people in the name of Jesus and to go back to the pits of hell of where it came from, never to return again, in the name of Jesus.

I declare that the joy of the Lord is their strength (Nehemiah 8:10).

I decree and declare that they are strong in You and in the power of Your might (Ephesians 6:10). I declare in the name of Jesus they shall have a crown of beauty instead of ashes, the oil of joy instead of mourning, and a garment of praise instead of a spirit of despair (Isaiah 61:3).

Thank You for turning their mourning into dancing and that they have the mind of Jesus Christ (Psalm 30:11).

I thank You, heavenly Father, that they shall have clear and organized thought patterns and clear and organized speech in the name of Jesus. I thank You, heavenly Father, for doing a creative miracle in their lives.

I thank You for healing their physical bodies and for performing creative miracles—healing and delivering them from strokes, heart attacks, type 1 and type 2 diabetes, cancer, lung disease, heart failure / cardiac arrest, high blood pressure, kidney diseases, and all physical healings they stand in need of in the name of Jesus. You are the bomb of Gilead, and we thank You, Jesus, for the shedding of Your blood that covers them, protects them, heals them, and delivers them from all matters of sickness and disease.

For You are Jehovah Rapha, the Lord God that heals them. You took up our infirmities and bore our diseases (Matthew 8:17). You are the great I Am that I Am, and there is nothing too hard for You to do! All things are possible with God in the name of Jesus!

Therefore, I declare that everything that the enemy meant for evil, you are turning around for their good (Genesis 50:20).

I thank You, heavenly Father, for the manifestation of every prayer and declaration. Let Your will be done in our lives according to Your Word. I give You all of the glory, honor, and praise this day. In Jesus's name. Amen!

# Personalize Your
## Prayers, Decrees & Declarations

---— D A Y —---

# 14

---

## SELF-ENCOURAGEMENT

### ADORATION

I delight in You, and I praise You each and every day! There is no God like my God. You are the great I Am that I Am. I praise You, Jehovah Nissi, my protector and my banner!

### CONFESSION

Heavenly Father, You said in Your Word, according to 1 John 1:9, if we confess our sins, You are faithful and just to forgive us our sins and to cleanse us from all unrighteousness. God, I'm sorry for falling short in _____ and that my actions in _____ haven't lived up to Your expectations. I repent for not doing_____ when I should have done_____ . Heavenly Father, I let go of all offense, bitterness, anger, and disappointment, and I release it all unto You. I forgive _____, who have hurt me, disappointed me, and caused me any harm. You said in Your Word to forgive other people when they sin against me so that You, heavenly Father, will also forgive me (Matthew 6:14). I receive Your forgiveness. I have no condemnation in Christ (Romans 8:1), and I thank You for helping me to do better the next time. In Jesus's name. Amen.

## Thanksgiving

I thank You, Father, for keeping me in perfect peace. You said in Your Word to be anxious for nothing but in everything by prayer and supplication and with thanksgiving, let your request be made known unto God (Philippians 4:6–). Thank You, heavenly Father, for the privilege and honor to come before Your throne. I thank You that You hear me each and every time I pray (1 Peter 3:12).

## Supplication

### Self-Encouragement

I decree and declare in the name of Jesus I am the head and not the tale, and I am above only and not beneath (Deuteronomy 28:13).

For I am fearfully and wonderfully made (Psalm 139:14)!

I decree and declare in the name of Jesus I am a mighty warrior. I am more than a conqueror through Jesus Christ who loved me (Romans 8:37). I overcome by the blood of the lamb and the word of my testimony (Revelation 12:11).

I decree and declare in the name of Jesus I cannot be stopped, and I cannot be denied because the promises of God are yes and amen (2 Corinthians 1:20).

I decree and declare in the name of Jesus Your supernatural favor for my life. You encamp around me as a shield of favor. My gifts are making room for me and bringing me before great men (Psalm 5:12; Proverbs 18:16).

As I decree a thing, it shall be established unto me (Job 22:28).

I decree and declare in the name of Jesus my words have power. When I speak to mountains, they move (Mark 11:23).

I decree and declare in the name of Jesus the angels of the Lord are on my side. The angels hearken to the voice of the Word of God as I open my mouth (Psalm 103:20).

I decree and declare in the name of Jesus that I am a child of the Most High God. Before You formed me in the womb, You knew me. Before I was born, You set me apart and appointed me as a prophet to the nations (Jeremiah 1:5). Your plans for me are good—plans not to harm me but to prosper me and give me a future and a hope (Jeremiah 29:11). Every hair on my head is numbered by You (Luke 12:7; Matthew 10:30). I pray in the name of Jesus that You keep me as the apple of Your eye (Psalm 17:8). I thank You, Lord, that You know my name and everything that concerns me and You rescue me.

I decree and declare in the name of Jesus I am accelerating, advancing, and moving forward. I press toward the mark of amazement—the high calling of God in Christ Jesus (Philippians 3:14).

I decree and declare in the name of Jesus I am called, equipped, and ready for battle with a double-edged sword in my mouth, declaring and decreeing the Word of God. I will stand in the gap and pray all kinds of prayers. I will make petitions, pray in the Spirit, and be alert with all perseverance for the saints and for all people (Hebrews 4:12; Ephesians 6:18).

I decree and declare in the name of Jesus that I am a chosen race, a royal priesthood, a holy nation, a people for God's own possession, so that I may proclaim the excellencies of He who has called me out of darkness into His marvelous light (1 Peter 2:9).

I decree and declare in the name of Jesus that I am unstoppable, steadfast, immoveable, always abounding in the work of the Lord, knowing that my toil is not in vain in the name of Jesus (1 Corinthians 15:58).

I thank You, God, that I am Your ambassador and representative of our Lord and Savior, Jesus Christ. I thank You for Your power, authority, and dominion that You have given me. I declare in the name of Jesus that power, demonstrations, miracles, signs, and wonders are supernaturally manifested and released unto others because of what I decree and declare according to the Word of God.

I decree and declare in the name of Jesus my hands are waring and my fingers and fighting to resist, interrupt, and renounce every evil work of the devil in the name of Jesus (Psalm 144:1).

I thank You, Lord, for blessing me. For the blessings of the Lord make me rich and add no sorrow. I decree and declare in the name of Jesus I am blessed, and whom God has blessed no man can curse. For I am the seed of Abraham, and the blessings of Abraham (being in right standing with God, walking with God, the favor of God, provision, protection, direction, help, and receiving the gift of the Holy Spirit by faith) are upon me. The king's heart is in Your hand, Lord, and I declare in the name of Jesus that You have turned it toward me (Proverbs 10:22; Numbers 22:12; Numbers 23:8; Isaiah 54:17; Romans 8:31; Mark 11:23; Deuteronomy 28:1–8; Galatians 3:14–29; Proverbs 21:1).

I decree and declare in the name of Jesus that the fruit of my womb is blessed. My children, children's children, and generations to come are advancing, prospering, enduring, persevering, praying, interceding, praising, worshiping, preaching, and teaching, with the compassion of Christ on all people, in the name of Jesus.

I decree and declare in the name of Jesus that the Spirit of the Lord is upon me. I am anointed to preach the Gospel accurately to the poor, to proclaim release to the captives and recovery of sight to the blind, to set free those who are oppressed and to proclaim the favorable year of the Lord (Isaiah 61: Luke 4:18–19).

I decree and declare in the name of Jesus I am reaching the lost and winning souls for the kingdom of God. With the Word of God, love, compassion, and a godly lifestyle, I am snatching them out of the fire (Jude 1:23). As You send me across their paths to witness the good news, the Gospel of Jesus Christ, I declare that they shall be saved. They shall receive Jesus Christ as their Lord and Savior and be filled and baptized with Your Holy Spirit and fire.

Father, in the name of Jesus, I thank You for Your Word. Thank You, Holy Spirit, for doing a great work inside of me. Thank You for stirring up the gifts of the Holy spirit within me and distributing them as You will and for Your purpose (1 Corinthians 12:8, 11). Thank You, Jesus. You are forever making intercessions for me (Hebrews 7:25). Let the words of my mouth and the mediation of my heart be acceptable in Your sight (Psalm 19:14). I thank You for hearing me and answering my prayer. I believe that I receive when I pray (Mark 11:24). Let Your will be done in my life according to Your holy Word. In Jesus's name. Amen.

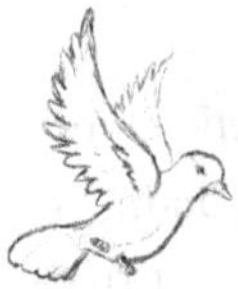

# Personalize Your Prayers, Decrees & Declarations

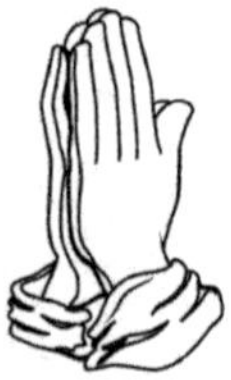

# 15

## THE PROMISES OF GOD

### ADORATION

Father, in the name of Jesus, I rejoice in You today! For You are an awesome God. You are my portion and the lover of my soul. I thank You that you are doing miraculous things in my life, in the lives of others, in this nation and this country! You are a victorious God who never loses a battle. You are El Elyon, the Most High God. I will bless the Lord at all times. His praise shall continually be in my mouth. For my God is a great God! His majesty reigns supreme forever and ever! Hallelujah! You are the bread of life, and it is written, "Man shall not live by bread alone, but by every word that proceeded out of the mouth of God. Hallelujah! I rejoice at Your Word as one who finds great spoils! And, seven times a day, I praise you because of Your righteous ordinances" (Psalm 119:162, 164; Psalm 93:1–2; Matthew 4:4).

### CONFESSION

Heavenly Father, You said in Your Word, according to 1 John 1:9, if we confess our sins, You are faithful and just to forgive us our sins and to cleanse us from all unrighteousness. God, I'm sorry for falling short in _____ and that my actions in _____ haven't lived up to Your expectations. I repent for not doing_____ when I should have done_____ . Heavenly Father, I let go of all offense, bitterness, anger, and disappointment, and I release it all unto You. I forgive _____, who have hurt

me, disappointed me, and caused me any harm. You said in Your Word to forgive other people when they sin against me so that You, heavenly Father, will also forgive me (Matthew 6:14). I receive Your forgiveness. I have no condemnation in Christ (Romans 8:1), and I thank You for helping me to do better the next time. In Jesus's name. Amen.

## Thanksgiving

I delight myself in You this day, and I enter into Your presence with rejoicing, thanksgiving, joy, and amazement. I thank You, Jesus, for Your unconditional love! You carried the cross for me, You died on the cross for me, You shed Your blood on the cross for me, You tore the veil in two for me, You took the keys of death and hell for me, and You rose again for me. You sent me Your Holy Spirit, and You are continuously interceding for me! Hallelujah! Thank You, Jesus!

## Supplication

## The Promises of God

For Your promises to me according to Your Word are always yes and amen (2 Corinthians 1:20)!

I will trust in the Lord with all my heart and lean not to my own understanding. In all of my ways, I will acknowledge Him, and He shall direct my paths. Some trust in chariots and horses, but I will trust and will always remember the name of the Lord (Proverbs 3:5–6; Psalm 20:7)!

I declare Isaiah 40:31 in the name of Jesus; as I wait upon the Lord, He shall renew my strength. I shall mount up on wings as eagles, I shall run and not be weary, and I shall walk and not faint.

I am strong and courageous. I will not be afraid or discouraged because the Lord my God is with me wherever I go (Joshua 1:9).

I will remain strong in the Lord and in the power of His might. I will keep on the whole armor of God, so that I am able to stand firm against the schemes of the devil (Ephesians 6:10–11).

I declare in the name of Jesus that I will be anxious for nothing, but in everything by prayer and supplication, with thanksgiving, I will let my requests be made known to God. And the peace of God, which surpasses all understanding, will guard my heart and mind through Christ Jesus (Philippians 4:6–7).

I decree and declare Romans 8:28, that God causes everything to work together for my good, because I love God and am called according to His purpose.

I thank You, Lord, and I give You praise. I thank You for showing Yourself strong through me. Thank You for opening up doors for me that no man can shut and closing doors that no man can open. I thank You that the manifestations of Your promises and blessings are continuing to evolve and become more evident within my life. For the blessings of the Lord maketh rich, and he adds no sorrow with it (Proverbs 10:22).

I declare in the name of Jesus that my God reigns, and He is Lord of lords and King of kings!

For nothing can stop the plans of God! You said in Your Word that Your plans for me are good, plans not to harm me but to prosper me and give me a future and a hope (Jeremiah 29:11).

Just as Paul and Silas prayed and sang praises unto God, and the prisoners heard them, and suddenly a great earthquake happened, and the foundations of the prison shook, and immediately all the doors opened, and everyone's bands were loosed, I declare and decree that as I continue to engage in prayer, praise, worship, and perseverance and help others in need, the anointing and the power of God will supernaturally change my situation, circumstances, and people. I declare and decree that God will supernaturally heal, deliver, and set free in the name of Jesus (Acts 16:25).

I thank You, Lord, for Your anointing upon me to fulfill my purpose and to sustain the blessings and promises of God.

I decree and declare in the name of Jesus that this is my year and my time of supernatural favor. I decree and declare in the name of Jesus that God is making all things new for me in my life. I decree and declare in the name of Jesus that I am walking into the promises of God. He is making my name great, my nation great, and He is showering down blessings upon me so that I am able to shower down blessings upon others (Genesis 12:2).

For I am the head and not the tail, above and not beneath (Deuteronomy 28:13)!

For I shall have what I say, and as I decree a thing, so shall it be unto me according to the supernatural and infallible Word of God! Therefore, I decree and declare salvation, healing, and deliverance to all humankind. May all see the goodness of the Lord in the land of the living. I decree and declare good success, great health, great wealth, and that I am living in the overflow and abundant blessings of the Most High God! Thanks be unto God for the manifestation of this prayer. In Jesus's name. Amen (Mark 11:23; Job 22:28; Psalm 27:13).

# Personalize Your
## Prayers, Decrees & Declarations

# 16

## PERSEVERANCE

### ADORATION

Father, in the name of Jesus, I come humbly before You, giving you honor, praise, and glory. You are a good God, and I love you, appreciate You, and adore You. There is none like You. My soul rejoices in You! "Bless the Lord, O my soul, and all that is within me, bless His Holy name. Bless the Lord, O my soul, and forget none of His benefits, Who pardons all your iniquities, Who heals all your diseases, Who redeems your life from the pit, Who crowns you with loving kindness and compassion, Who satisfies your years with good things, So that your youth is renewed like the eagle" (Psalm 103:1–5).

### CONFESSION

Heavenly Father, You said in Your Word, according to 1 John 1:9, if we confess our sins, You are faithful and just to forgive us our sins and to cleanse us from all unrighteousness. God, I'm sorry for falling short in _____ and that my actions in _____ haven't lived up to Your expectations. I repent for not doing_____ when I should have done_____ . Heavenly Father, I let go of all offense, bitterness, anger, and disappointment, and I release it all unto You. I forgive _____, who have hurt me, disappointed me, and caused me any harm. You said in Your Word to forgive other people when they sin against me so that You, heavenly Father, will also forgive me (Matthew 6:14). I receive Your forgiveness. I have no

condemnation in Christ (Romans 8:1), and I thank You for helping me to do better the next time. In Jesus's name. Amen.

## THANKSGIVING

I thank You for the loving-kindness You have shown me throughout my life. For the loving-kindness of the Lord is from everlasting to everlasting on those who fear Him, and His righteousness to children's children, to those who keep His covenant and remember His precepts to do them. I thank You for Your holy Word. I thank You for healing, deliverance, and salvation in Your Word. I thank You for speaking to me through Your Word, leading me through Your Word, giving me clarity and direction through Your Word, and for blessing me through Your Word (Psalm 103:17–18).

Your Word is a lamp to my feet and a light unto my path, and it is the final authority of all of the affairs of my life. For in the beginning was the Word, and the Word was with God, and the Word was God. I thank You that the Word became flesh and that it dwells among me and that I am able to behold Your glory. I thank You that the living Word of God is on the inside of me, dwelling among me richly with all wisdom in my spirit and in my mouth (Psalm 119:105; John 1:1; John 1:14; Colossians 3:16).

## SUPPLICATION

### PERSEVERANCE

I thank You, Father, that You hasten to Your Word to perform it (Jeremiah 1:12)!

Your angels are harkening to the voice of the Word of the Lord when I pray, and You are faithful to do what You have promised (Psalm 103:20; Hebrews 10:23).

I believe that I receive each and every time I pray because I know that You always hear me (Mark 11:24; Psalm 116:2).

I come boldly before Your throne with confidence. I have confidence that whatsoever I ask according to Your will, you hear me, and because I know that You hear me, I know that I have the petitions that I have desired of you (1 John 5:14–15).

I will continue to stand victorious and in expectancy when I pray.

You said in Your Word, according to Isaiah 65:24, that before I call, You will answer, and while I am still speaking, You will hear.

For You are near to all who call upon You and to all who call upon You in truth (Psalm 145:18).

I will not grow weary in well doing. I know that at the proper time, I will reap a harvest if I do not give up (Galatians 6:9).

For it is God's will that by doing good, I put to silence the ignorance of foolish men (1 Peter 2:15).

I declare that I will fight the good fight of faith and endure hardship as a good soldier of Jesus Christ (1Timothy 6:12)!

I will not be ignorant or distracted by the enemy's devices. I will do good and listen to the Lord like Gideon and demonstrate the sharpness and alertness, just like Gideon's three hundred men who lapped water with their hands to their mouths. And just like Nehemiah's servants who held spears, shields, bows, and armor as they returned to rebuild the wall (Judges 7:4–7; Nehemiah 4:15–17). For this cause, I will be sober, vigilant, and alert because I know that my adversary, the devil, prowls around as a roaring lion, seeking someone to devour. But I will resist him and will stand firm in my faith and in the knowledge that the same kinds of afflictions and sufferings are being experienced by my brothers and sisters throughout the world (1 Peter 5:8–9).

I declare in the name of Jesus that I will continuously submit myself unto God, resist the devil, and he will flee. I will draw nigh to God, and He will draw nigh to me (James 4:7–8).

Hallelujah! I magnify your name, God, and I give you a *ruwa* praise (praises of shouting and rejoicing that split the ears of the enemy)!

I will not break rank. I will count it all joy through various trials and tribulations, because I know that the testing of my faith produces perseverance. Therefore, I will let perseverance finish its work, so that I may be mature and complete, not lacking anything (James 1:2–4).

For I know and understand that my light affliction, which is but for a moment, worketh for me, a far more exceeding and eternal weight of glory (2 Corinthians 4:17).

For many are the afflictions of the righteous, but the Lord, Jehovah MePhalti, delivers me out of them all (Psalm 34:19).

For Your Word tells me in 1 Peter 5:10, after I have suffered a little while, the God of all grace, who called me to His eternal glory in Christ, will perfect, confirm, strengthen, and establish me.

Therefore, I declare that I am strong in You and in the power of Your might (Ephesians 6:10)!

I will be steadfast, immovable, always abounding in the work of the Lord, knowing that my labor is not in vain in the Lord (1 Corinthians 15:58).

Thanks be unto God, who gives me the victory through my Lord, Jesus Christ (1 Corinthians 15:57!

I have guaranteed victory in Christ Jesus! I shall rejoice, sing, dance, and celebrate my victory in the winner's circle! Lord, I thank You for fulfilling every promise and for answering this prayer. In Jesus's name. Amen.

# Personalize Your
## Prayers, Decrees & Declarations

# 17

## Spiritual Warfare
## Spiritual Leaders
## Healing for the Body of Christ

### Adoration

I bless Your great and mighty name because You are the God who never changes. You are the same yesterday, today, and forevermore (Hebrews 13:8). You are dependable, and You are trustworthy! You are my strong tower, my refuge, and my strength. You are my great defender and my protector. For the Lord is good, a stronghold in the day of trouble, and He knows those who take refuge in Him (Nahum 1:7). I love You, and I trust you. I adore You because You are my heavenly Father. You are always providing and are always looking ahead and making provision for me. You are always healing, delivering, forever saving and setting the captives free!

### Confession

Heavenly Father, You said in Your Word, according to 1 John 1:9, if we confess our sins, You are faithful and just to forgive us our sins and to cleanse us from all unrighteousness. God, I'm sorry for falling short in _____ and that my actions in _____ haven't lived up to Your expectations. I

repent for not doing_____ when I should have done_____
. Heavenly Father, I let go of all offense, bitterness, anger, and disappointment, and I release it all unto You. I forgive _____, who have hurt me, disappointed me, and caused me any harm. You said in Your Word to forgive other people when they sin against me so that You, heavenly Father, will also forgive me (Matthew 6:14). I receive Your forgiveness. I have no condemnation in Christ (Romans 8:1), and I thank You for helping me to do better the next time. In Jesus's name. Amen.

## THANKSGIVING

I thank You for my life, my health, and my strength. I don't take You for granted, and I do not take Your Word for granted. I thank You for Your anointing. For it is the power of God and the anointing of God that destroys every yoke and sets the captives free (Isaiah 10:27)!

## SUPPLICATION

## SPIRITUAL WARFARE

As I enter Your gates with thanksgiving and Your courts with praise, I acknowledge Your supreme authority and sovereignty (Psalm 100:4). I thank You for giving Your only begotten Son, Jesus Christ, to die on the cross for my sins. I thank You, Father, for sending me Your Helper, the Holy Spirit. I thank You for the blood of Jesus Christ that sanctifies me, covers me, and protects me.

Father, in the name of Jesus, I plead the blood of Jesus Christ over my children, grandchildren, family members, spouse, coworkers, unsaved friends and unsaved loved ones, myself, finances, employment, transportation, and everything that pertains to me in the name of Jesus. I declare that no evil shall befall us, and no plague shall come near our dwelling place. I declare that the angels of the Lord are taking charge concerning us and are guarding us in all of our ways (Psalm 91:10–11).

I bind up principalities, powers, and the rulers of the darkness and spiritual wickedness in high places that You have given me jurisdiction over in the name of Jesus. I loose forth the Word of God according to Luke 10:19, that You have given me the authority to trample on snakes and scorpions and to overcome all the power of the enemy, and nothing will harm me.

I take authority and bind up the diabolical spiritual force of Jezebel that seeks to divide, cause strife, retaliate, falsely accuse, lie, conquer, deceive, murder, and corrupt God's leaders and those around them. I overthrow, dismantle, and utterly destroy with the fire of God and the blood of Jesus Christ, its plan to cause disruption and hindrance, as I operate in the prophetic, strategic prayer and intercession in the name of Jesus!

I thank You, Lord, for giving me the power and authority to bind and to loose. For whatever I bind on earth is bound in heaven, and whatever I loose on earth will be loosed in heaven (Matthew 18:18).

Therefore, I bind up and arrest the spirits of doubt, fear, unbelief, unforgiveness, hatred, bitterness, rejection, self-rejection, greed, resentment, offensiveness, anger, rage, terroristic attacks, murder, strife, prejudice, racism, discord, chaos, division, and mayhem in the jurisdiction that You have given me authority over in the name of Jesus Christ. I loose forth the love of God, the peace of God, and the Word of God in the name of Jesus.

For the love of God covers a multitude of sins. I declare the peace of God that surpasses all understanding shall guard our hearts and our minds in Christ Jesus (1 Peter 4:8; Philippians 4:7).

You did not give me the spirit of fear but of power, love, and a sound mind in the name of Jesus (2 Timothy 1:7).

I take authority in the name of Jesus Christ, and I loose forth the Word of God, which is spirit and life and is quick, powerful, and sharper than any two-edged sword, piercing even to the dividing asunder of soul and spirit, and of the joints and marrow, and is a discerner of the thoughts and intents of the heart (Hebrews 4:12; John 6:63).

Father, in the name of Jesus, I bring before You my unsaved loved ones and those on this earth who are not saved, who are living in sin, and who are practicing sexual immorality.

Father, in the name of Jesus Christ of Nazareth, I plead the blood of Jesus Christ over them. I call their names out (name them) continuously before You, and I declare the Word of God over them, that they will confess with their mouth Jesus is Lord and will believe in their hearts that God raised Him from the dead, and they will be saved (Romans 10:9).

I bind up any and all matters of confusion within their minds, and I loose forth clarity within their minds in the name of Jesus. I declare total healing of past hurts, trauma, exploitation, abuse, and neglect in the name of Jesus. I declare in the name of Jesus total deliverance of any involvement of drug and alcohol addiction, occults, curses, bewitchment, and false religion.

I declare in the name of Jesus that You are continually sending forth divine labors across their pathway. I thank You, God, for continually setting up divine appointments for the Gospel of Jesus Christ to be ministered to them. I pray that they will accept and receive Jesus Christ as their Lord and Savior and will be filled and baptized with Your Holy Spirit and fire.

For this purpose, the Son of God was manifested, that He might destroy the works of the devil (1 John 3:8). I declare and decree that the works of the devil are destroyed concerning every aspect of my life (health, children, home, marriage, ministry, relationships, finances, business, etc.) in the name of Jesus.

I will not be moved by what I see, hear, or feel. I pray from a position of dominion and authority and with victory and defeat over the enemy. I take a hold of my dominion and authority, and I pray!

I pray without ceasing, and I build myself up, and I pray in my most holy faith (1 Thessalonians 5:16; Jude 1:20)!

I pray in the Spirit on all occasions with all kinds of prayers and requests (Ephesians 6:18).

I am alert and will always keep on praying for all the Lord's people.

As I stand on God's Word and in the name of Jesus, the devil must flee, and he has to obey me because I do not waver in my faith! I am not a weak Christian! I am not lukewarm! I am a minister of flames of fire (Psalm 104:4)!

I have the power of the Holy Spirit inside of me to take authority over any demonic influence in the name of Jesus!

Greater is He who is inside of me than he who is in the world (1 John 4:4).

I believe the Word of God, and I walk in faith without wavering in the name of Jesus!

The power of God's Holy Spirit empowers me for victorious living in the name of Jesus!

As a child of God, I have authority and power over all devils because it is exercised in my faith in Jesus Christ.

I love You, praise You, and worship You, Jesus! Your Holy Spirit is in me and is ready to move as You allow, to take authority over devils.

For the name of Jesus is more powerful than all devils.

Therefore, I speak to my situations and to the devil, and he must bow down at the name of Jesus, the name above every name!

Hallelujah, I praise Your holy name, Jesus!

I will persevere in the faith, war in the spirit, resist the enemy, and refute and interrupt every lie and scheme of the devil and his imps. I will renounce every unproductive and negative thought and voice of the enemy. I will fight the good fight of faith. I will be strong and courageous in the Lord, and I will win in the name of Jesus (1 Timothy 6:12; Joshua 1:9)!

I decree and declare that I always win, and I always triumph in the name of Jesus (1 Corinthians 15:57)!

I will not fear, for the Lord is with me. I will not be dismayed, for God is my God! He will strengthen me and help me. He will uphold me with His righteous right hand (Isaiah 41:10).

I thank You that I am moving forward and taking ground with a double-edged sword in my mouth to defeat my giants.

I declare that Jesus Christ is Lord! The effectual and fervent prayers of the righteous are effective and make tremendous power available, in the name of Jesus (James 5:16).

## Spiritual Leaders

Hallelujah and all praise be unto our Lord and Savior, Jesus Christ! I lift up to You, heavenly Father, my spiritual leaders today. I ask that You give my leaders Your spirit of wisdom and revelation in the deep, intimate, full knowledge of You. I pray that their eyes and their hearts and understanding will continue to be enlightened and flooded with light, so that they might know what is the hope of their calling and the riches of the glory of Your inheritance in them. I pray in the name of Jesus for the exceeding greatness of Your power toward them, because they believe according to the working of Your mighty power that You wrought in Christ when You raised Him from the dead and set Him at Your own right hand in the heavenly places (Ephesians 1:17–20).

I declare in the name of Jesus that the spirit of the Lord will continue to rest on our leaders—the spirit of wisdom and understanding, the spirit of counsel and might and strength, the spirit of knowledge, and of the reverence and obedient fear of the Lord (Isaiah 11:2).

Father, in the name of Jesus, I pray that You grant the manifestation of the Spirit to be given to them and to profit them in all that they do in the name of Jesus: the word of wisdom, the word of knowledge, faith, gifts of healing, the working of miracles, prophecy, discerning of spirits, diverse kinds of tongues, and interpretation of tongues (1 Corinthians 12:7–10).

Father, You are the Most High God. You are the one who appoints. You are the one who calls and equips. You, magnificent God, are the one who builds up and tears down, who exalts and who humbles.

I thank You for Your sovereignty, Your mercy, and Your grace.

I thank You for covering our leaders this day with Your love, joy, peace, safety, and protection.

I plead the blood of Jesus over our leaders and declare that if You are for them, You are more than the whole world who is against them.

For Your Word says that when the enemy comes in like a flood, the spirit of the Lord will lift up a standard against him (Isaiah 59:19).

I thank You, Jehovah Nissi, for being our standard (our armed resistance with the Word of God) against any tactics the enemy may try to infiltrate against our leaders.

I bind and rebuke the enemy's plans to kill, steal, and destroy, and I put him to flight in the name of Jesus (John 10:10)!

I declare that the gates of hell shall not prevail against our leaders in the name of Jesus (Matthew 16:18)!

I sever and disannul the spirits of fear, doubt, unbelief, deception, self-condemnation, anxiety, temptation, sickness, and disease in the regions that you have given us jurisdiction of in the name of Jesus.

I declare that our leaders are loosed and set free and are walking in the fullness and the glory of God.

For whom the Son has set free is free in deed in the name of Jesus (John 8:36)!

For they are the redeemed of the Lord in the name of Jesus (Psalm 107:2)!

I declare that our leaders have the mind of Jesus Christ and that they are strong in You and the power of Your might (Ephesians 6:10)!

I declare in the name of Jesus, above all things, they shall prosper and be in good health as their souls prosper (3 John 1:2)!

I come against sickness and disease, and I bind and rebuke the spirit of infirmity in the name of Jesus.

I declare in the name of Jesus that Jesus took their infirmities and bore their sicknesses on the cross (Matthew 8:17).

I decree and declare in the name of Jesus that by the stripes of Jesus, our leaders are healed. For healing is the children's bread. Our leaders are the healed and not the sick, in the name of Jesus (Isaiah 53:5; Matthew 15:26).

I decree and declare that God is restoring to them health and will heal their wounds (Jeremiah 30:17).

Thank You for restoring to them health and letting them live (Isaiah 38:16–17).

For our leaders shall walk in total prosperity of the king in the name of Jesus!

## Healing for the Body of Christ

I lift up to You the body of Christ. I bind and rebuke every evil assignment and attack on the body of Christ concerning our healing and deliverance.

I plead the blood of Jesus over every member of my church (name your church), our partners, members of our affiliated churches, and every church representative and member.

I decree and declare that the works of the devil are destroyed! I resist, interrupt, and renounce sickness and disease in the name of Jesus.

I arrest the trespassing spirit of infirmity, and I cast it out of our bodies and command it to leave and go back to the pits of hell of where it came from, never to return again, in the name of Jesus.

I speak to our bodies and command them to line up to the Word of God and function the way God created them to function.

I declare that we were created in the perfect image and likeness of God (Genesis 1:27).

I believe the report of the Lord concerning our healing! You sent Your Word to heal us and deliver us from all of our destruction (Psalm 107:20)!

With the Word of God and the releasing of my faith, I exercise my power, authority, and dominion given to me by God Almighty, in the name of Jesus.

I speak life to our mortal bodies, and I speak life to those around me who are battling sickness and disease.

I speak to sickness and disease and declare that it cannot stay in our bodies in the name of Jesus.

I decree and declare in the name of Jesus that our bodies are the temples of the Holy Spirit (1 Corinthians 6:19–20).

I decree and declare in the name of Jesus that we shall not die but live and declare the works of the Lord (Psalm 118:17).

For You came to give us life, and life more than abundantly, in the name of Jesus (John 10:10).

By faith in my Lord and Savior, Jesus Christ, and by the power of God's

Holy Spirit, I use my tongue to speak, declare, and take authority over the spirit of infirmity in the name of Jesus.

I command sickness, disease, stroke, cancer, diabetes, heart problems, cardiovascular disease, and high blood pressure to bow down at the name of Jesus.

I cast out the spirit of inheritance of stroke and the death of brain cells in the name of Jesus. I speak to the brain and command all blockage to dissolve and be removed. I command all damaged tissue to be restored in the name of Jesus. I command a creative miracle and a new brain in the name of Jesus.

I bind and cast out the spirit of cancer in the name of Jesus. I curse the seed, root, and cells of cancer in the name of Jesus. I speak to every affected area within our bodies, and I command every cancer cell in our bodies to dry up and die in the name of Jesus. I command the bone marrow to produce pure, healthy blood in the name of Jesus. I command healing in the name of Jesus to all organs and tissues affected and restore every part of the body where it needs to be restored in the name of Jesus. I declare in the name of Jesus for every good cell within our bodies to seek out and destroy every bad cell. I command the body's defensive killer cells to multiply and attack every cancer cell in the name of Jesus.

I speak to diabetes, and I cast out the spirits of inheritance in the name of Jesus. I command and speak forth a new pancreas into our bodies in the name of Jesus. I command any damaged body parts due to excess sugar to be healed, restored, and made whole in the name of Jesus!

I speak to cardiovascular disease and heart problems in the name of Jesus. I speak a new heart into our bodies in the name of Jesus. I command a creative miracle in the name of Jesus. I speak to our arms, and I command our arms to grow out and for all other parts of our bodies affected by heart disease to be healed in the name of Jesus.

High blood pressure, I speak to you in the name of Jesus. I command a divine roto-rooter treatment throughout the entire vascular system in the name of Jesus. I command the blood pressure to return to normal and to remain normal in the name of Jesus.

I declare in the name of Jesus and by the power of God's Holy Spirit a creative miracle within our bodies.

I speak to every organ, every tissue, and every cell within our bodies, and I command them to be healed and to line up according to the Word of God in the name of Jesus!

I command every good cell within our bodies to utterly seek out and destroy every bad cell within our bodies in the name of Jesus.

I command the electrical and chemical frequencies within our bodies to be in perfect harmony, balance, and alignment, in the name of Jesus.

I command every bone, tendon, muscle, and joint within our bodies to be strengthened and lengthened in the name of Jesus. I command all pain to go away and disappear. I command pain to be removed and cast into the sea, never to return again, in the name of Jesus. Wherever there is any misalignment in our arms and legs, I speak forth a creative miracle. I command our arms and legs to grow out and to be in perfect alignment in the name of Jesus.

I command our immune systems to be strong, healthy, and vibrant and to function normally in the name of Jesus.

I command all bitterness, anger, resentment, failure, disappointment, rejection, self-rejection, hatred, self-hatred, and fear that are the contributing factors of such spirits of infirmity and diseases to be broken off of us and to flee from our bodies, minds, and spirits now in the name of Jesus.

In the name of Jesus, and by the power of God's Holy Spirit, deliver and set us free. I thank You for sending forth Your Word to heal us and to deliver us from all destruction, in the mighty name of Jesus!

I thank You, Father, that You satisfy our mouth with good things, so that our youth is being renewed like an eagle's (Psalm 103:5).

Daily, You load our mouths with benefits (Psalm 68:19). For Your Word is life to those who find them and health to one's whole body (Proverbs 4:22).

Your Word is actively pursuing its destiny, to which I have directed it to go. You said in Your Word that if I decree a thing, it shall be established unto me (Job 22:28). You also said that Your Word does not return unto You void (when I speak, decree, declare, and pray it); instead, it accomplishes everything that You have sent it to do (Isaiah 55:11).

The angels of the Lord are harkening to the voice of Your Word (Psalm 103:20).

Your Word is manifesting the presence of the Holy Spirit around us and on the inside of us, and the devil's ailments of sickness and disease are fleeing from us now in the name of Jesus.

I decree and declare in the name of Jesus that Your Word and Your presence are setting us free from demonic oppression, possession, and depression, healing and delivering our bodies and our minds, and we are set free in the name of Jesus!

For who the Son sets free is free in deed in the name of Jesus (John 8:36).

Hallelujah! I declare that we are free for real because of the shed blood of Jesus Christ. For the shedding of the blood of Jesus Christ is for the remission of our sins.

Thank You for the ultimate price You paid for our lives, and because You laid down Your life for us and went to the Father, we have the Holy Spirit!

I thank You, heavenly Father, that Your Word is transforming the lives of people in need of a tangible touch from You. Surely. God, You have listened and attended to the voice of my prayer (Psalm 66:19). For this, I praise You and magnify Your name. Thank You for honoring and fulfilling Your Word according to every prayer and declaration that has gone forth this day. In Jesus's name. Amen.

# Personalize Your
## Prayers, Decrees & Declarations

# 18

## SUPERNATURAL MIRACLES
## HOLY SPIRIT
## EMPLOYMENT AND FINANCES

### ADORATION

I thank You for the opportunity each and every day to walk with You. I appreciate my fellowship and my relationship with You. I thank You that as I continue to walk with You, I will continue to experience Your supernatural mercy, grace, and favor. You are Jehovah Jireh, my provider and Jehovah Raah, my shepherd. Nothing and no one can compare to who You are—Your superiority, sovereignty, and supernatural being.

### CONFESSION

Heavenly Father, You said in Your Word, according to 1 John 1:9, if we confess our sins, You are faithful and just to forgive us our sins and to cleanse us from all unrighteousness. God, I'm sorry for falling short in _____ and that my actions in _____ haven't lived up to Your expectations. I repent for not doing_____ when I should have done_____ . Heavenly Father, I let go of all offense, bitterness, anger, and disappointment, and I release it all unto You. I forgive _____, who have hurt

me, disappointed me, and caused me any harm. You said in Your Word to forgive other people when they sin against me so that You, heavenly Father, will also forgive me (Matthew 6:14). I receive Your forgiveness. I have no condemnation in Christ (Romans 8:1), and I thank You for helping me to do better the next time. In Jesus's name. Amen.

## THANKSGIVING

I thank You for being an awesome God who is always speaking to me through Your Word and for giving me direction and instruction through Your Word. I thank You for speaking to me in my dreams, giving me visions, showing me what and who to pray for, and giving me fresh revelation knowledge concerning Your Word. I praise Your great and mighty name! For You said in Your Word that in these last days, "I will pour out My Spirit on all people." Your sons and daughters will prophesy, Your young men will see visions, your old men will dream dreams (Acts 2:17). I thank you for the supernatural manifestation of Your Word with miracles, signs, and wonders.

## SUPPLICATION

### SUPERNATURAL MIRACLES, HOLY SPIRIT

Holy Spirit, I thank You for leading me and guiding me through prayer. Your Word says, according to Romans 8:26–27, "In the same way the Spirit also helps our weakness; for we do not know what to pray for as we should, but the Spirit Himself intercedes for us with groanings too deep for words; And he who searches our hearts knows the mind of the Spirit, because the Spirit intercedes for God's people in accordance with the will of God." So be it unto me according to Your Word.

Father, in the name of Jesus, I acknowledge that Your Holy Spirit is not here to satisfy our ego, to attract attention to ourselves, or to engage in any fleshly excitement or emotional self-indulgence.

I approach Your throne with clean hands and a pure heart and with all genuine humility, adoration, reverence, and respect. For You are holy.

In the name of Jesus and by the power of God's Holy Spirit, I bind and rebuke the diabolical spirits of pride, false humility, and any unclean, foul spirit that would open the way for a satanic counterfeit or demonic activity within my midst.

I plead the blood of Jesus over myself, my body, family members, children, marriage, spouse, finances, employment, ministry, and everything that pertains to me. I cancel every evil assignment of the enemy as I go forth during and after prayer and intercession, decreeing and declaring the Word of God in the name of Jesus.

I decree and declare in the name of Jesus that there will be no backlash or retaliation from the enemy in the name of Jesus. For one will put a thousand to flight, and two will put ten thousand to flight (Deuteronomy 32:30; Joshua 23:10; Isaiah 30:17; Psalm 91:7).

I decree and declare in the name of Jesus that You have given me power and authority to tread on serpents and scorpions and power over all of the enemy, and nothing by any means shall harm me, in the name of Jesus (Luke 10:19).

I decree and declare in the name of Jesus the power of God's Holy Spirit is a consuming and holy fire (a sign of God's power, presence, passion, purity, and judgment), and it is utterly burning up and destroying every evil plot, scheme, and plan of the enemy.

I decree and declare in the name of Jesus that our God is a consuming fire (Hebrews 12:29), and His Holy Spirit will come down upon Your people as a consuming fire and will be a sign of Your glory, as it is written in Leviticus 9:23, "Fire came out from before the Lord and consumed the burnt offering and the fat on the Altar. When the people saw it, they shouted and fell on their faces."

I decree and declare in the name of Jesus that Almighty God, the Father, Son, and the Holy Spirit, will come down among us as a consuming fire (His presence and Shekinah glory) even as I go forward in prayer and in unity with other believers and pray just like Solomon:

> When Solomon had finished praying at the dedication of the temple, fire came down from heaven and consumed the burnt offering and the sacrifices; and the glory of the Lord filled the temple. And the priest could not enter the house of the Lord, because the glory of the Lord had filled the Lord's house. (2 Chronicles 7:1–2)

I thank you, God, for Your Holy Spirit. I thank You that You are forever with me. I thank You that every time I touch heaven with my prayers, You come down upon me and fill me with Your glory as a consuming fire, just as Elijah prayed on Mount Carmel:

> The fire of the Lord fell and consumed the burnt sacrifice, and the wood and the stones and the dust licked up the water that was in the trench. Now when all the people saw it, they fell on their faces and they said, "The Lord, He is God!, The Lord, He is God!"

I decree and declare in the name of Jesus that every time I have an encounter with God, it will be a sign to the believer and the unbeliever that my God is the only true and Living God. He is master! He is Lord! He is King of kings and Lord of lords! Those who have fallen away from the faith (backsliders) and those who are not saved will repent and believe in Jesus as their Lord and Savior. They shall be filled and entrenched in Your presence as an all-consuming fire!

I decree and declare in the name of Jesus that the power of God will take me into a deeper work of the Holy Spirit in order for God's message to come full of life and power, sharper than a two-edged sword to cause an awakening, true repentance, and a harvest of souls (Hebrews 4:12).

I decree and declare in the name of Jesus that just as Peter stood up in the power of the Holy Spirit, three thousand souls were saved, and after that, five thousand souls were saved after he preached the Gospel. So be it unto me as I go forward to preach, teach, and spread the Gospel. Let me do so in the power of the Holy Spirit and with holy boldness to turn stony hearts to hearts of flesh for the sake of repentance, salvation, and receiving the gift of the Holy Spirit.

For Peter said to them, "Repent and each of you, be baptized in the name of Jesus Christ for the forgiveness of your sins, and you will receive the gift of the Holy Spirit" (Acts 2:38).

I decree and declare in the name of Jesus that the power of God's Holy Spirit will cause both believers and unbelievers to turn away from sin and toward doing the work of righteousness and holiness in the name of Jesus.

For the Holy Spirit is our helper and the Spirit of truth. John 14:16–17 states, "And I will pray the Father, and He will give you another Helper, that He may abide with you forever-the Spirit of Truth, whom the world cannot receive, because it neither sees Him nor knows Him, but you know Him, for He dwells with you and will be in you."

I decree and declare in the name of Jesus that the Holy Spirit will help us, comfort us, meet our needs, and give us fresh revelation knowledge.

For the Holy Spirit is the revelator and the interpreter of God's Word to us.

I decree and declare in the name of Jesus that the helper, the Holy Spirit, whom the Father has sent in Jesus's name, will teach me all things and bring into remembrance all things Jesus said unto me (John 14:26).

I decree and declare in the name of Jesus, John 14:6, Jesus is the truth, and God's Word is truth, according to John 17:17. Furthermore, I decree and declare 1 John 5:6; the Holy Spirit is truth, and He is reigning inside of me.

I decree and declare in the name of Jesus the threefold presentation of truth (God the Father, the Son, Jesus Christ, and the Holy Spirit) gives me the power to save the lost, heal the sick, raise the dead, cast out devils, operate in the supernatural, and preach and teach the Gospel effectively, with the power and demonstration of miracles, signs, and wonders.

I decree and declare in the name of Jesus, as I preach and teach the Gospel of Jesus Christ, it will be done not only in word but in power and in the Holy Spirit and in much assurance (1 Thessalonians 1:5).

I decree and declare in the name of Jesus I have the power of the Holy Spirit inside of me to be His witnesses across the world (Acts 2:8).

I decree and declare in the name of Jesus that as I go about doing my Father's business, He is with me. "You know how Jesus of Nazareth, how God anointed Him with the Holy Spirit and with power, and how He went about doing good and healing all who were oppressed by the devil, for God was with Him" (Acts 10:38). So be it unto me in the name of Jesus!

I decree and declare in the name of Jesus I will not forget that, as a Christian, a New Testament born-again believer, I have been enlightened, have tasted the heavenly gift, have been made a partaker of the Holy Spirit, and have tasted the good Word of God and the powers of the age to come (Hebrews 6:4–6).

I decree and declare in the name of Jesus I will not forget that God has made a down payment, a deposit (*arrhabon*, Hebrew) in me, and He is coming back for His prize possession!

I was included in Christ when I heard the Word of truth, the Gospel of my salvation. Having believed, I was marked in Him with a seal, the promised Holy Spirit, who is a deposit guaranteeing my inheritance until the redemption of those who are God's possession, the praise of His glory (Ephesians 1:13–14).

I decree and declare in the name of Jesus that until my redemption draws nigh, I will continue to occupy, study, show myself approved, and operate in the ministry gifts of the Holy Spirit that He has called me to with the supernatural power and ability of Almighty God. I will be about my Father's business until He returns.

I decree and declare in the name of Jesus that my teaching, preaching, praying, ministering, and living will be supernaturally empowered, transformed, protected, and directed by the power of God's Holy Spirit.

I decree and declare in the name of Jesus that as I glorify Jesus, submit myself unto God through prayer, fasting, praise, worship, studying the Word of God, having faith, and obeying in the Word of God, live a godly lifestyle, and remain sensitive and obedient to the Holy Spirit, God will supernaturally use me to perform extraordinary miracles by my hands and by my very presence in the name of Jesus.

"And God was performing extraordinary miracles by the hands of Paul" (Acts 19:11). "People brought the sick into the streets and laid them on beds and mats so that at least Peter's shadow might fall on some of them as he passed by" (Acts 5:15). So be it unto me in the name of Jesus that God will continue to endow me with the ministry gifts of His Holy Spirit as He wills, to release His Glory through my hands and my very presence.

I decree and declare in the name of Jesus, because I am filled with the Holy Spirit, dry bones will awaken and come to life, and when I lay hands on the sick, they shall recover. The eyes of the blind will be opened, and the ears of the deaf will be unstopped. The lame will leap like a deer. and the mute tongue will shout for joy. Demons will flee, and spirits of infirmity will be no more, in the name of Jesus (Ezekiel 37:5–10; Mark 16:18; Mark 10:46–52; Mark 7:30–37; John 5:1–9; Matthew 9:31–33; Mark 5:1–20; Luke 8:43–48; Mark 5:25–34; Matthew 9:20–22; Isaiah 35:6).

I thank You, Father God, that by Your power and gift of the Holy Spirit, I will walk into my promised land with silver and gold, and there will be no feeble person among me (Psalm 105:37).

Hallelujah! I thank You, God, for the new wine that was already provided for us by the working of the power of God's Holy Spirit. New order, new inspiration, new manifestation, and new revelation knowledge straight from the throne of God.

I decree and declare in the name of Jesus that because God has filled me with His Holy Spirit, there is a freshness, beauty, and quality about me that will create in others the desire for the same.

I decree and declare in the name of Jesus I am filled with the power of God's Holy Spirit. I burst forth with fresh energy and new rivers and fresh, living water flowing from within me. I take Jesus at His word because He said, "He who believes in Me, as the scripture said, from his innermost being (out of our bellies) will flow rivers of living water" (John 7:38).

As a partaker of the divine nature and through the power of God's Holy Spirit, I will manifest the life of Jesus Christ to the world.

I cultivate the nature of the lamb. I will not grieve the Holy Spirit of God, whom I was sealed from the day of redemption. I get rid of all bitterness, rage and anger, brawling and slander, along with every form of malice. I will be kind and compassionate and forgiving, just as in Christ God forgave me (Ephesians 4:30–32).

I will demonstrate the love of God to all humankind. The love of God is shed abroad in my heart by the Holy Ghost, which was given to me (Romans 5:5).

I thank You, Holy Spirit, for Your supernatural power that exists to exalt Jesus, to convict men and women of their sins, righteousness, and judgment, and to write God's law into their hearts and bring them into a new way of living, and to produce miracles.

## Supernatural Miracles

You are the God of miracles. According to Psalm 77:14, You are the God who performs miracles. You display Your power among the people and through Your people.

For You are El Shaadi, God Almighty, and You can do the impossible!

I declare in the name of Jesus that I have the anointing, the authority, and the power of God's Holy Spirit to speak, decree, and declare miracles.

Heavenly Father, I thank You for Your anointing and the power of Your Holy Spirit to perform miracles!

You are holy, and I reverence Your presence. Holy Spirit, I yield to You. You are our master, and You are our Lord. You are the Most High God, the only true and Living God. There are no other gods before You. You are the great I Am that I Am.

I thank You, God, for providing me with the Holy Spirit to work miracles because I hear and believe Your Word by faith in the name of Jesus (Galatians 3:5).

I thank You for a great salvation and that You testify to me and through me by signs and wonders, by various miracles, and by the gifts of the Holy Spirit as You will (Hebrews 2:4).

I declare in the name of Jesus that utterance may be given to me in the opening of my mouth to make known with boldness the mystery of the Gospel (Ephesians 6:19).

I thank You that the creation of the church through the preaching of the Gospel will display Your presence and glory, to proclaim the manifold wisdom of God to the nations and to the rulers and authorities in the heavenly places.

According to Ephesians 3:10–11, "His intent was that now, through the church, the manifold wisdom of God (the cross, Jesus Christ made of God unto us wisdom, righteousness, sanctification, and redemption) should be made known to the rulers and authorities in the heavenly realms, according to the eternal purpose that He accomplished in Christ Jesus our Lord."

I declare in the name of Jesus that the manifold wisdom of God will be revealed to nations through the kingdom of God in me. For the kingdom of God is within me, and I declare that His presence and His glory will be revealed to all humankind through the distribution of the gifts of the Holy Spirit (the word of wisdom, word of knowledge, faith, gifts of healing, working of miracles, prophecy, distinguishing of spirits, various kinds of tongues, interpretation of tongues) as He wills, and through the fivefold ministry of apostles, prophets, evangelists, pastors, and teachers, for the equipping of the saints for the work of service, to build up the body of Christ, to do mighty exploits, and to represent heaven on Earth!

I decree and declare in the name of Jesus there is nothing too hard for You to do. You are able to do exceedingly and abundantly above that I can ask or think according to the power that works in me (Jeremiah 32:27; Ephesians 3:20).

I declare in the name of Jesus I am strong in You, Lord, and in the power of Your might. Where I am weak, Jesus, You make me strong. It is in God that I live, move, and have my eternal being (Ephesians 6:10; 2 Corinthians 12:10; Acts 17:28)!

I thank You, God, for Yeshu'a. For Yeshu'a is my salvation, deliverance, welfare, prosperity, and victory.

I thank You for being a supernatural God!

I expect my heavenly Father to do supernatural things on my behalf and

His people, just like He redeemed and restored the people of Israel from their exile in Babylon, according to Psalm 107:35–37:

> For You changed a wilderness into a pool of water, and a dry land into springs of water—and in that place, you made the hungry dwell in it, so that they may establish an inhabited city, and sow fields and plant vineyards, and gather a fruitful harvest. And You blessed them so that they could multiply greatly and prevent their cattle from decreasing!

> So be it unto me according to Your Word!

I thank You for redeeming me, restoring me, blessing me, and multiplying everything that you have blessed me with.

Therefore, I will continue to declare out of my mouth and will stand on the promises and prophecies of God from the beginning, according to Genesis 12:2–3:

> You will make us into a great nation, and You will bless Us;
> You will make our name great, and we will be a blessing.
> You will bless those who bless us, and whoever curses us,
> You will curse; and all peoples on earth will be blessed
> through us.

I decree and declare in the name of Jesus Deuteronomy 1:10. You O' God, will continue to increase my numbers (my seed, my population) so that I will be as numerous as the stars in the sky.

I decree and declare in the name of Jesus Deuteronomy 7:14. I will be blessed more than any other people, and none of our men or women will be childless, nor will any of our livestock be without young.

I thank You, Father, that You will continue to shower down Your blessings upon me, so that I will be able to shower down blessings upon others in the name of Jesus (Ezekiel 32:26)!

I decree and declare a bountiful harvest coming my way in the name of Jesus (Leviticus 25:19–29). I call it forth from the north, the south, the east, and the west, and I thank You, Lord, for being the God of miracles, the God of increase, and the God who hears and answers prayer. I thank You,

Jesus, for salvation and the harvest of souls coming into the kingdom of God through the working of Your supernatural miracles. Thank You, Jesus, for the manifestation of this prayer. So be it unto me according to Your Word. In Jesus's name. Amen.

# Personalize Your
## Prayers, Decrees & Declarations

---- D A Y ----

# 19

---

## Spiritual Warfare

### Adoration

Forever, O Lord, Your Word is settled in heaven. Your faithfulness continues throughout all generations. You established the earth, and it stands. They stand this day according to Your ordinances, for all things are Your servants. If Your law had not been my delight, then I would have perished in my affliction. I will never forget Your precepts, for by them You have revived me (Psalm 119:89–93).

### Confession

Heavenly Father, You said in Your Word, according to 1 John 1:9, if we confess our sins, You are faithful and just to forgive us our sins and to cleanse us from all unrighteousness. God, I'm sorry for falling short in _____ and that my actions in _____ haven't lived up to Your expectations. I repent for not doing_____ when I should have done_____. Heavenly Father, I let go of all offense, bitterness, anger, and disappointment, and I release it all unto You. I forgive _____, who have hurt me, disappointed me, and caused me any harm. You said in Your Word to forgive other people when they sin against me so that You, heavenly Father, will also forgive me (Matthew 6:14). I receive Your forgiveness. I have no condemnation in Christ (Romans 8:1), and I thank You for helping me to do better the next time. In Jesus's name. Amen.

## Thanksgiving

Father, in the name of Jesus, I thank You for allowing me to see another day and for granting me the privilege and honor to be able to come before Your presence. Thank You for being my healer, my deliverer, and the horn of my salvation.

Thank You, Jesus, for being a lamp unto my feet and a light unto our path (Psalm 119:105). For You are the Word of God and the bread of life (John 1:14; John 6:35)!

I thank You, God, for our Lord and Savior, Jesus Christ, who died on the cross for my sins. I thank You that there is now no self-condemnation for those who are in Christ Jesus.

I thank You for the blood of Jesus. I thank You that my heart is sprinkled and purified by the blood of Jesus from an evil consciousness (Hebrew 10:22).

Therefore, I break the power of sin and iniquity in my life through the blood of Jesus. As I come before You with clean hands and a pure heart, with the anointing and power of the Holy Spirit, I take dominion and authority, and I release and declare out of my mouth the Word of God. For I shall not live by bread alone but by every Word of God that proceeds out of my mouth.

So I open up my mouth today to thank You and to declare Your goodness, Your mercy, Your favor, Your grace, Your protection, and Your peace that You have already bestowed upon me according to Your written and Rhema Word. I thank You for the manifestation of Your promises and prophecies and that it is coming to pass. It is coming to pass for my seed, my lineage, my family, my future, and years to come.

A good man leaves an inheritance for his children's children, and the wealth of the wicked is laid up for the just (Proverbs 13:22).

I thank You for opening up the floodgates of heaven and pouring blessings upon me without measure (Malachi 3:10).

I thank You for the outpouring of Your blessings, that they will shower down upon me so that we can shower down blessings upon others (Ezekiel 34:26).

I thank You for Your favor, for Your Word says that surely You will bless the righteous and encamp around him like a shield of favor (Psalm 5:12).

Hallelujah, I praise You, I magnify You, I exalt You, because You are a good Father!

You never fail me, You never lie, You never stop loving me, You never stop fighting for me, and You said in Your Word that You will never leave me or forsake me.

I take You at Your Word that You are always mindful of me. You are causing Your face to shine down upon me. You are upholding me with your righteous right hand. I thank You for leading me, guiding me, shaping me, and molding me into Your image and likeness to be a light to the world, salt to the earth, a repairer of the breach, a restorer of the streets, a minister of reconciliation, and a minister as flames or fire (Psalm 115:12; Numbers 6:24–26; Isaiah 41:10; Isaiah 58:12; Matthew 5:13–16; Isaiah 58:12; 2 Corinthians 5:11–21; Hebrews 1:7; Psalm 104:4;).

I thank You, Father, for making me Your vessel of honor and conduit of Your Word and for equipping me and anointing me with Your power, authority, and Holy Spirit with fire, to demonstrate your gifts of the Spirit and fruit of the Spirit.

I thank You, Father, that as I decrease and humble myself, You will continue to increase within me Your wisdom and fill me with Your Holy Spirit and fire in the name of Jesus.

I thank You that as I yield my mouth, my mind, my will, my intellect, and my emotions unto You, out of my belly will continue to flow living streams of water. I thank You for Your anointing that destroys every yoke and for the supernatural outpouring of Your Holy Spirit to be able to minister effectively before the masses—to preach, to cast out devils, to heal the sick, to raise the dead, to baptize with water, and to minister the baptism of the Holy Spirit with fire, with the evidence of speaking tongues (Matthew 28:16–20; Luke 24:44–49; Mark 16:14–18; Acts 1:8; John 20:19–23).

I thank You, Father, for teaching my hands to war and my fingers to fight. I thank you for strengthening me with Your power and Your might (Colossians 1:11). I will keep my armor on and continue to use my spiritual weapons as I fight the good fight of faith in the name of Jesus (1 Timothy 6:12).

## SUPPLICATION

### SPIRITUAL WARFARE

I declare in the name of Jesus that if You, Father God, are for me, You are more than the whole world against me (Romans 8:31).

As I continue to decree and declare the Word of God, stand on the Word of God, Have faith, trust, and believe the Word of God, plead the blood of Jesus, and exalt the name of Jesus, the gates of hell shall not prevail against me!

I decree and declare in the name of Jesus that You, O God, will thunder upon my enemies through the release of Your voice, Your Word, with hailstones and coals and fire in the name of Jesus (Psalm 18:13).

I thank You, Jehovah Mephalti, for delivering me from my strong enemy and from they who are too strong for me (Psalm 18:17).

I thank You that You have given me the power to tread upon serpents and scorpions and over all the power of the enemy, and nothing shall by any means hurt me (Luke 10:9).

For You have given me the neck of my enemies, and I will utterly destroy and disannul them in the name of Jesus (Psalm 18:40).

No more mediocracy.

No more delay.

No more distractions.

No more disappointments.

No more manipulation.

No more controlling spirits or people.

No more slander.

No more spirits of haughtiness, pride, rivalry, and competition.

No more bullying.

No more conspiracy.

I say no, and I arrest these spirits in the name of Jesus! I take authority and command these spirits to burn up and die by the fire of God in the name of Jesus!

Let every plan of the enemy to kill, steal, and destroy fail in the name of Jesus.

Let God arise and my enemies be scattered in seven ways in the name of Jesus (Deuteronomy 28:7)!

I bind and cast out the strong man and every thief who would try to steal my joy, peace, healing, wealth, and deliverance, in the name of Jesus (John 10:10).

I declare the Word of the Lord of Hosts, according to Malachi 3:11, that You, Father God, will rebuke the devour for my sake, and the enemy shall not destroy the fruit of my grounds, and neither shall my vine cast her fruit before the time in the field in the name of Jesus!

Hallelujah! I know You will come through for me! I will not doubt because a double-minded man is unstable in all of his ways (James 1:8)!

I will not forget the name of the Lord! I will remember the name of the Lord, Jehovah Nissi, our banner, Jehovah Mephalti, our deliverer, Jehovah Jireh, our provider, Jehovah Shalom, our peace, Jehovah Sabaoth, the Lord of hosts, and You are the Lord who opens doors for me!

I thank You for baptizing me with Your Holy Ghost and fire in the name of Jesus and that You are continually filling me with your Holy Spirit, wisdom, and faith.

I thank You that as I continue to walk with You and meditate on Your Word day and night, I will continue to prosper, and I will continue to increase in wisdom, stature, and favor with God and man in the name of Jesus (Psalm 1:1–3; Luke 2:52)!

I will operate in my gifts, talents, and calling as a minister of flames of fire and with the anointing, power, and authority of the Most High God!

I shall do mighty exploits because I know my God!

I will not look out for my own interests but for the interests of others (Philippians 2:4)!

I will lift up my brothers and sisters in Christ, in the name of Jesus!

Nothing will be done through strife or vainglory, but in lowliness of mind I will esteem others better than myself (Philippians 2:3).

For two is better than one (Ecclesiastes 4:9)!

Iron sharpens iron as one man sharpens another (Proverbs 27:17)!

I decree and declare in the name of Jesus that I will work together to be about our Father's business, in the name of Jesus (Luke 2:49)!

One will put a thousand to flight, and two will put away ten thousand (Deuteronomy 32:30)!

With my brothers and sisters in Christ, together we will run through troops and leap over walls (Psalm 18:29)!

With my brothers and sisters in Christ, together we will shout down the walls of Jericho (Joshua 6:20)!

With my brothers and sisters in Christ, together we will slay our Goliaths (1 Samuel 17:50)!

With my brothers and sisters in Christ, together, as we come in agreement in the name of Jesus, anything that we ask our Father in heaven, that thing, whatever we need Him to do, He will do, in the name of Jesus Christ of Nazareth (Matthew 18:19)!

For God is faithful to fulfill His promise, and His promises to me are always yes and amen (Hebrews 10:23)!

His Word does not return to me void; it accomplishes everything He sent it to do. He hastens to His Word to perform it, and the angels of the Lord harken to the voice of the Word of God as I release it out of my mouth, in the name of Jesus (Isaiah 55:11; Jeremiah 1:12; Psalm 103:20)!

I declare in the name of Jesus that no matter what it looks like, I will not be moved by what I see, how I feel, or what I hear.

I decree and declare in the name of Jesus that I will walk by faith and not by sight, because Your Word tells me that it is nothing but faith that pleases the Father (2 Corinthians 5:7; Hebrews 11:6).

I decree and declare in the name of Jesus that I will only be moved by the Word of God, and I will only believe the report of the Lord in the name of Jesus (Isaiah 51:3)!

And Your report is always good! I will be like Joshua and Caleb. I will come out and come back with a good report, and I will move out and be courageous and take the land (Numbers 13–14)! For I am more than a conqueror through Jesus Christ in the name of Jesus (Romans 8:37)!

Your Word tells me that if I have faith the size of a mustard seed, I can say to the mountain, "Move from here to there," and it will move, and nothing will be impossible for me (Matthew 17:20).

Therefore, I speak to the mountain of doubt, unbelief, fear, failure, setbacks, and disappointments, and I command you to move in the name of Jesus!

I speak to the mountain of infirmity, sickness, and disease, and I command it to move out of the midst of my life in the name of Jesus!

Sickness and disease have no place in my body, for I am the healed and not the sick! I speak to every limb, every muscle, every tendon, every nerve, every cell, every organ, every tissue, and my mind—the faculties of my mind, my thought processes and thought patterns—I command it to be clear in the name of Jesus.

I cast out every vain thought of suicide, depression, and low self-esteem and every imagination consisting of auditory and visual hallucinations and delusions that exalt themselves against the knowledge of God, and we bring it into the obedience of Jesus Christ (2 Corinthians 10:5).

I command my body and my mind to be healed and to line up to the Word of God in the name of Jesus.

I declare that Jesus Christ was wounded for our transgressions and bruised for our iniquities, and the chastisement of our peace was upon Him, and by His stripes we were healed in the name of Jesus Christ of Nazareth (Isaiah 53:5)!

Hallelujah. He already made things new for me in the name of Jesus! No matter what it looks like, I declare a new body and a new and renewed mind in the name of Jesus!

Hallelujah, let this mind be in you, which was also in Christ Jesus (Philippians 2:5)! Hallelujah!

I declare that the old man is dead, that it is no longer I who live but Jesus Christ who lives on the inside of me (Galatians 2:20). It's a new day. It's a new year! It's an amazing day! It's an amazing year! And if our God is for me, who can be against me!

I am stepping all the way into the promises and prophecies of God, and there is nothing that the devil or people can do or say to stop it!

For the fire of God propels me and protects me, and the blood of Jesus protects me, covers me, anoints me, heals me, delivers me, purifies me, and sanctifies me as I move forward into my promised land in the name of Jesus!

I declare in the name of Jesus that I am moving into a place flowing with milk and honey, and as I keep my focus up above, I will enter into a holy city, the new Jerusalem, coming down out of heaven from God, and God's dwelling place will be among His people, and He will dwell with them. He will wipe away every tear from my eyes, and there will be no more death, no more mourning or crying or pain, because the older order of things has passed away (Revelation 21:1–4)!

Hallelujah, I am occupying until Jesus comes, and when Jesus comes, I will be ready in the name of Jesus!

You Word tells me that I can call those things that be not as though they were (Romans 4:17).

Your Word tells me that faith is the substance of things hoped for and the evidence of things not seen (Hebrews 11:1).

Therefore, I stand on Your Word in faith, in the name of Jesus! "And it was by faith even Sarah, who was past childbearing age, was enabled to bear children because she considered him faithful who had made the promise" (Hebrews 11:11).

Hallelujah! I thank You, Father, that You are an amazing God and that You have already set in motion everything You promised, prophesied, and ordained for me.

I take You at Your Word!

I declare in the name of Jesus that I will work together in unity with all born-again believers, all Christian churches across the world, the body of Christ, and of all ages, cultures, and nationalities. We will take this world back and be like those who turned the world upside down because of the love, unity, and forgiveness and the anointing, power, and authority of the Gospel of Jesus Christ being preached by your people—with signs, miracles, and wonders to follow.

I thank You for unity in the body of Christ, both internally and externally. I thank You that there are no little I's and big You's in the love of Jesus Christ. For we are all God's children! "For God so loved the world, that he gave his only and begotten son, and whosoever believes in him, will not perish, but will have everlasting life" (John 3:16).

I thank You, Father, for the mercy, grace, and unmerited love and Father that You have bestowed upon all of humankind.

I humble myself before You! For You are the Most High God! You are the one who makes my name great. My titles and my positions are nothing and mean nothing if You are not in it and if You are not at the center of every motive, intention, and execution of every work I set my hands to do!

For Jesus said, "I am the vine, you are the branches and he who abides in Me and I in him, he bears much fruit, for apart from Me you can do nothing" (John 15:5).

Lord, help me to abide in You and not in my own works so that I can bear much fruit, in the name of Jesus.

I declare in the name of Jesus that as I abide in the master, I will not become distracted, deceived, or confused by the enemy.

I will open my mouth in defiance of every plot, plan, and scheme of the devil, in the name of Jesus, and I bind up the spirit of jealousy, envy, strife, gossip, discord, lies, false accusations, conspiracy, and retaliation in the jurisdiction that You have given me authority over in the name of Jesus.

For where envy and strife are, there *is* confusion and every evil work (James 3:16). Therefore, I take authority over the atmosphere and every region you have given me jurisdiction over, and I utterly destroy every evil work of the enemy, and I command jealousy, pride, envy, strife, gossip, discord, division, lies, false accusations, conspiracy, backbiting, all distractions, deception, and the spirit of confusion to burn up and die by the fire of God.

Father, shut the mouths of lions and silence their lying lips—those proud and arrogant lips that accuse the godly (Psalm 31:18). Let their tongues stick to the roof of their mouths in the name of Jesus (Ezekiel 3:26).

I take authority, and I bind up the diabolical spiritual force of Jezebel that seeks to divide, cause strife, retaliate, falsely accuse, lie, conquer, deceive, murder, and corrupt our lives, our families, our children, the body of Christ, God's leaders, and those around them. I overthrow, dismantle, and utterly destroy with the fire of God and the blood of Jesus Christ its plan to cause a disruption and hindrance, as I operate in prophetic, strategic prayer and intercession in the name of Jesus!

Father, in the name of Jesus, set a guard over my mouth and keep watch over the doors of my lips (Psalm 141:3).

I will let no unwholesome talk come out of my mouth but only what is helpful for building up the one in need and bringing grace to those who listen (Ephesians 4:29) in the name of Jesus.

I declare in the name of Jesus that my mouth is filled with your praise, declaring Your splendor all day long and declaring that You, O God, will exceed my wildest dreams this year and that we will be ready in the name of Jesus (Psalm 71:8).

We declare that everything I say and do, when I open up my mouth and declare the Word of God and do the works of the Lord, is all being done for the glory of God!

I will not forget about the treasures and wealth that You have given me and that are in hidden places. For every good and perfect gift comes from above (James 1:17). You are always mindful of me. And You are a God who is always more than enough and always shows Yourself strong and mighty through me, just like You did for the widow who owed her creditor and who was about to have her two sons taken as slaves. All she had was a small jar of olive oil. But You blessed what she had and caused it to increase and overflow to pay off the debt and still live in the overflow with her sons (2 Kings 4:1–7).

So be it unto me according to Your Word, that You bless what I have, increase it, and cause it to overflow, because you are such a marvelous, phenomenal, breathtaking, amazing, barrier- breaking, and supernatural God!

For God *is* able to make all grace abound toward us, that we may always have all sufficiency in all *things*, so that we may abound to every good work (2 Corinthians 9:8).

For as I put my trust in God, I will not be made ashamed (Romans 10:11).

I decree and declare in the name of Jesus that the Lord shall bless me and keep me. He shall make His face shine upon me and continue to be gracious to me. He will lift up His countenance upon me and give me peace (Numbers 6:24–26).

For You are a faithful God, and You always come through.

There is no God like our God! I bless Your great name! Thank You for the manifestation of this prayer. In Jesus's name. Amen.

# Personalize Your
## Prayers, Decrees & Declarations

# 20

## Finances

## Marriages

## For Those Who Are Single

### Adoration

I love You, Lord, and I appreciate Your loving-kindness toward me each and every day. You are the saving strength of Your people and the saving refuge of Your anointed (Psalm 28:8).

### Confession

Heavenly Father, You said in Your Word, according to 1 John 1:9, if we confess our sins, You are faithful and just to forgive us our sins and to cleanse us from all unrighteousness. God, I'm sorry for falling short in _____ and that my actions in _____ haven't lived up to Your expectations. I repent for not doing_____ when I should have done_____ . Heavenly Father, I let go of all offense, bitterness, anger, and disappointment, and I release it all unto You. I forgive _____, who have hurt me, disappointed me, and caused me any harm. You said in Your Word to forgive other people when they sin against me so that You, heavenly Father, will also forgive me (Matthew 6:14). I receive Your forgiveness. I have no

condemnation in Christ (Romans 8:1), and I thank You for helping me to do better the next time. In Jesus's name. Amen.

## THANKSGIVING

I thank You, Lord, for being my strength. I sing praises to You of your strength and of Your steadfast love in the morning. For You, O' God, are the one who girds me with strength and makes my way blameless. For the joy of the Lord is my strength! I thank You for Your strength and Your love, because it took great strength and love to give me Your only begotten Son, Jesus Christ, to die on the cross for my sins and to set me free. Thank You for sustaining me with Your Word and girding me with Your power and might. It's in You that I live, move, and have my eternal being (Psalm 59:16; Psalm 18:32; Nehemiah 8:10; Acts 17:28).

## SUPPLICATION

### FINANCES

Father, in the name of Jesus, thank You for allowing me to move forward and advance in faith and in great expectancy of the acceleration of every prayer, decree, declaration, promise, and prophecy that You have spoken over my life according to Your Word.

Hallelujah! I praise Your name, Jesus, for being mindful of me, for saving me, for delivering me, for healing me, for blessing me, for increasing me, and for bringing me into a wealthy place of abundance!

In the name of Jesus and by the power of God's Holy Spirit, I declare a financial breakthrough in my life. You, Jehovah Jireh, know exactly what I stand in need of, and I trust You for sending forth Your Word to supernaturally provide me with unexpected staters (pieces of money) to pay every debt. Jesus directed Peter to "go to the sea and throw in a hook, and take the first fish that comes up and when you open its mouth, you will find a piece of money. Take that and give it to them for Me and yourself." So be it unto me according to Your Word.

For it is not Your will for me to owe any man a debt except to love him. I declare in the name of Jesus that God is supernaturally making a way for me to be a lender and not a borrower, according to His Word (Romans 13:8; Deuteronomy 15:6; Deuteronomy 28:12).

I decree and declare in the name of Jesus, for the Lord my God will bless me as He has promised me, and I will lend to many nations, but I will not borrow. I will rule over many nations, but they will not rule over me (Deuteronomy 15:6).

I decree and declare in the name of Jesus that the Lord will open for me His good storehouse, the heavens, to give rain to my land in its season and to bless all the work of my hand, and I shall lend to many nations, but I shall not borrow (Deuteronomy 28:12).

I decree and declare in the name of Jesus, the Lord my God, Jehovah Jireh is working everything out for me. He supplies all of my needs according to His riches and glory in Christ Jesus (Philippians 4:19).

I decree and declare in the name of Jesus the blessings of the Lord are overtaking me and I am living in the overflow. For the blessings of the Lord makes me rich, and it adds no sorrow because I am living in the promises and prophecies of Almighty God (Proverbs 10:22)!

I decree and declare in the name of Jesus that I am living in the overflow! My barns are filled to overflowing, and my vats are brimming with new wine (Proverbs 3:10).

I declare in the name of Jesus the Lord is making all grace abound toward me with all sufficiency so that I will have abundance for every good work (2 Corinthians 9:8).

Wealth and riches shall be in my household. I am blessed because I am a doer of Your Word. I am willing and obedient, and therefore I shall eat the good of the land (Psalm 112:3; Isaiah 1:19; James 1:25).

My children shall be successful everywhere. They are the generation of the upright, and I am blessed. I am blessed by the Lord, the maker of heaven and earth. For the heavens are the heavens of the Lord (Psalm 115:15)!

You are a good God! I shall see the goodness of the Lord in the land of the living, and with long life, You will satisfy me and show me Your salvation (Psalm 27:13; 91:16).

You are the God of miracles! Thank You for doing a miracle in my finances.

You are the God of increase! Thank You for increasing my finances and for giving me the favor, mindset, wisdom, and obedience to be a good steward over my financial increase, in the name of Jesus (Luke 2:52).

You give me power to obtain wealth (Deuteronomy 8:18)!

For You are omniscient. You are all-knowing, and You teach me to profit (Isaiah 48:17)!

Thank You for opening up the floodgates of heaven and pouring out blessings upon me where I don't have room enough to receive it. I thank You for rebuking the devour for my sake in Jesus's name (Malachi 3:10–12).

I decree and declare in the name of Jesus the curse of poverty, lack, and debt is broken over my life. I lack no good thing in You. For all the animals of the forest are Yours, and You own the cattle on a thousand hills (Psalm 34:10; Psalm 50:10).

For every good and perfect gift comes from above, coming down from the Father of the heavenly lights, who does not change like shifting shadows (James 1:17). I thank You, and I receive Your Word concerning my finances. So be it unto me according to Your Word. In Jesus's name. Amen.

## MARRIAGES

Father, in the name of Jesus, I thank You for marriages. Marriage between a man and a woman is honorable before the Lord. Father, in the name of Jesus, I declare unity within my marriage. "Therefore what God has joined together, let not man separate" (Matthew 19:5–6).

According to Genesis 2:24 and Matthew 19:5, therefore shall a man leave his father and his mother and shall cleave unto his wife, and they shall be one flesh.

I decree and declare in the name of Jesus Ecclesiastes 4:12. My marriage is like a cord of three strands and cannot be easily broken.

I decree and declare in the name of Jesus Ephesians 4:2–3. Jesus is at the center of my marriage. With all humility and gentleness and patience, husband and wives will bear with one another in love, eager to maintain the unity of the Spirit in the bond of peace.

I decree and declare in the name of Jesus Colossians 3:14. My marriage is filled with the unconditional love of Christ. "And over all these virtues that husbands and wives will put on love, which binds them all together in perfect unity."

I decree and declare in the name of Jesus honor and commitment are respected and valued in my marriage. We will live together in love. The husband will love his wife as Christ loved the church and gave Himself up for her, according to Ephesians 5:25.

I decree and declare in the name of Jesus Ecclesiastes 9:9. My marriage is filled with the joy of the Lord. For Your Word says the husband shall live joyfully with his wife, whom he loves. I decree and declare in the name of Jesus Proverbs 5:18. The husband is blessed as he rejoices in the wife of his youth.

I decree and declare in the name of Jesus that husbands will love their wives and will not be harsh with them, according to Your Word in Colossians 3:19.

I decree and declare in the name of Jesus 1 Corinthians 7:3. The husband will fulfill his marital duty to his wife, and likewise the wife to her husband.

I decree and declare in the name of Jesus Ephesians 5:22–24. Wives will submit themselves to their own husbands as unto the Lord. The husband is the head of the wife even as Christ is the head of the church, His body, and Himself, its Savior. Now as the church submits to Christ, so also wives should submit in everything to their husbands.

I decree and declare in the name of Jesus 1 Peter 3:1–5. Wives will be subject to their own husbands, so that even if some do not obey the Word, they may be won without a word by the conduct of their wives, when they see the wives respectful and pure conduct.

I decree and declare in the name of Jesus Ephesians 5:21. Husbands and wives will submit themselves to each other out of reverence for Christ.

In the name of Jesus Christ and by the power of God's Holy Spirt, I come against and disannul the spirits of physical abuse, emotional abuse, sexual abuse, financial abuse, division, strife, selfishness, jealously, poor self-esteem, insecurity, sexual immorality, infidelity, adultery, lying, cheating, and covetousness in marriages. I plead the blood of Jesus Christ of Nazareth over our marriages, and I loose forth the peace of God according to His Word over husbands and wives and marriages in need of healing and restoration. In Jesus's name. Amen.

Peace I leave with you, and my peace saith the Lord, I give you, according to John 14:27.

I decree and declare in the name of Jesus that the peace of God, which surpasses all understanding, shall guard every husband's and wife's heart and mind in Christ Jesus, according to Philippians 4:7.

I decree and declare in the name of Jesus Numbers 6:24–26. The Lord blesses our marriages and keeps our marriages, the Lord makes His face shine upon our marriages and is gracious to our marriages, and the Lord lifts up His countenance upon our marriages and gives our marriages peace.

I decree and declare in the name of Jesus, for every husband and wife, according to Psalm 122:7, that peace be within their walls and security within their towers.

I decree and declare that the wonderful counselor, mighty God, everlasting Father, and Prince of Peace be with every husband and wife according to Your Word in Isaiah 9:7. So be it unto every husband and wife and within their marriages. In Jesus's name. Amen!

## For Those Who Are Single

I thank You, Lord, that Your timing is always perfect. Your Word says he who finds a wife finds a good thing and obtains favor from the Lord (Proverbs 18:22).

I decree and declare in the name of Jesus that as I trust in the Lord, I will find new strength. I will soar high on wings like eagles. I will run and not grow weary. I will walk and not faint (Psalm 40:31).

My body is the temple of the Holy Spirit. I was bought with a price. I will submit myself unto God and resist the devil, and he will flee (1 Corinthians 6:19; James 4:7).

For Your Word says those who wait for the Lord shall renew their strength; they shall mount up with wings like eagles; they shall run and not be weary; they shall walk and not faint (Isaiah 40:31).

I decree and declare in the name of Jesus that my heart will be content in all situations during this season (Philippians 4:11).

I decree and declare in the name of Jesus that I have a love for the Lord that consumes all of my heart. I will love the Lord my God with all my heart and with all my soul and with all my mind and with all my strength (Matthew 22:37).

The Holy Spirit will enable me to keep my heart with all diligence, for out of it flows the issue of life (Proverbs 4:23).

I will remain focused on the Lord, and I will walk by faith and not by sight (2 Corinthians 5:7).

I will trust in the Lord with all of my heart and lean not on my own understanding. In all my ways, I will acknowledge Him, and He shall direct my paths (Proverbs 3:5–6).

Thank You, Jesus, for Your unconditional love toward me and for Your presence abiding in me. I thank You, Lord, that as I delight myself in You, You will give me the desires of my heart (Psalm 37:4). So be it unto me and for those I have prayed for according to Your Word. In Jesus's name. Amen.

# Personalize Your
## Prayers, Decrees & Declarations

# 21

## Personal Encouragement
## Holy Spirit Working of Miracles

### Adoration

Hallelujah! I exalt Your name! El Sha-di, the Most High God, Adonai, Lord and master. I worship You in spirit and in truth. For You are omnipotent, all-powerful, omnipresent, everywhere at the same time, and You are omniscient. You are all-knowing. I reverence Your superiority over all, for your Word is upright, and all of Your works are done in faithfulness (Psalm 33:4).

### Confession

Heavenly Father, You said in Your Word, according to 1 John 1:9, if we confess our sins, You are faithful and just to forgive us our sins and to cleanse us from all unrighteousness. God, I'm sorry for falling short in _____ and that my actions in _____ haven't lived up to Your expectations. I repent for not doing_____ when I should have done_____ . Heavenly Father, I let go of all offense, bitterness, anger, and disappointment, and I release it all unto You. I forgive _____, who have hurt me, disappointed me, and caused me any harm. You said in Your Word to forgive other people when they sin against me so that You, heavenly Father, will also forgive me (Matthew 6:14). I receive Your forgiveness. I have no

condemnation in Christ (Romans 8:1), and I thank You for helping me to do better the next time. In Jesus's name. Amen.

## Thanksgiving

I thank You for the outpouring of Your Holy Spirit and with fire upon me. I thank You for filling me with Your presence and consuming my mouth with Your Word of life. I thank You for the written and Rhema Word of God that has been released into my life through the supernatural manifestation of the Holy Spirit concerning every promise and prophecy that You have proclaimed for my life.

## Supplication

## Personal Encouragement

I declare in the name of Jesus that as I open my mouth to declare and release the Word of God and speak to others in psalms, hymns, and making melody with my heart to the Lord, I will edify, exhort, and comfort others (Ephesians 5:19). For iron sharpens iron as one man sharpens another (Proverbs 27:17).

For You said in Your Word in Isaiah 26:3 that You will keep me in perfect peace, whose mind is stayed on Thee, because I trust in Thee.

You remind me in Philippians 4:8 that whatever is true, whatever is noble, whatever is right, whatever is pure, whatever is lovely, whatever is admirable—if anything is excellent or praiseworthy—to think about such things.

Therefore, I decree and declare that I will not be distracted. I will remain diligent and steadfast in Your Word to advance the kingdom of God.

I will be about my Father's business. I will be wise and save souls (Proverbs 11:30).

I will pursue my God-given destiny. I will take everything that God has set before me, and I will not leave this earth without using every gift and talent that You have given me.

I am a kingdom carrier and God's weapon of war (Luke 17:21; Jeremiah 51:20)!

I thank You for the manifestations of all nine gifts of the Holy Spirit operating through me as You will.

I press toward the mark for the prize of the high calling of God in Christ Jesus (Philippians 3:14)!

I thank You for the love of God that has been shed abroad my heart by the Holy Spirit! I thank You for sharpening my spiritual weapons through faith and obedience, prayer and intercession, the name of Jesus, the blood of Jesus, being in agreement, binding and loosing, fasting, praise, and the Word of God.

For the weapons of my warfare are not carnal but are mighty through God to the pulling down of strongholds!

I decree and declare that all strongholds against my family, spouse, marriage, children, grandchildren, great-grandchildren, neighbors, coworkers, church, ministry, business, and work, are utterly destroyed in the name of Jesus.

I decree and declare Your Word in the name of Jesus, 1 John 3:8. For this reason, the Son of God was made manifest (visible), that He might undo, destroy, loosen, and dissolve the works of the devil. I decree and declare that the works of Jesus Christ on the cross utterly destroyed the works of the devil, and the enemy is defeated.

For it is written, "Do not be afraid, I am the first and the last, and the living One; and I was dead, and behold, I am alive forevermore, and I have the keys of death and of Hades" (Revelation 1:18).

Therefore, sickness and disease have no hold on me, my marriage, family, children, grand-children, work, business, everything that pertains to me, and the gates of hell shall not prevail against us, in the name of Jesus (Matthew 16:18).

Your love for me on the cross defeated and utterly destroyed the works of the devil.

He himself bore my sins in His body on the cross, so that I might die to sin and live to righteousness, for by His wounds I was healed (1 Peter 2:24).

I thank You for the blood of Jesus Christ that was shed for me on Calvary and the love of God that covers a multitude of sins, saves to the uttermost, never fails, heals, delivers, sets me free, clothes me, feeds me, protects me, and is always mindful of me.

For You are a God who never slumbers or sleeps (Psalm 121:4).

You know the very number of hairs on my head (Luke 12:7).

I am the apple of Your eye, and I thank You, heavenly Father (Psalm 17:8)!

## Prayer and Declarations for Those
## Going through a Challenging Time

I lift up to You those who are going through challenging and difficult times. For Your Word says that You are near to the brokenhearted, You save those who are crushed in spirit, and You provide
rest for the weary (Psalm 34:18; Matthew 11:28–30).

Your Word says, "Come unto Me all who are weary and heavy-laden, and I will give you rest. Take my yoke upon you and learn from Me, for I am gentle and humble in heart, and you will find rest for your souls. For my yoke is easy and my burden is light" (Matthew 11:28–30).

I thank You for giving Your people rest and peace on this day. I decree and declare in the name of Jesus that You will give them the peace of God that surpasses all understanding and will guard hearts and mind in Christ Jesus.

I thank You for comforting them with your presence. For Your Word says that where the Spirit of the Lord is, there is liberty and freedom (2 Corinthians 3:17). I decree and declare in the name of Jesus that they are free from depression, fear, worry, and anxiety in the name of Jesus.

I cast out the spirit of depression in the name of Jesus and command that spirit to go back to the pits of hell of where it came from and to never return again, in the name of Jesus.

For You did not give your people a spirit of fear but of power, love, and a sound mind. I decree and declare in the name of Jesus that they will not be anxious for anything, but in every situation, by prayer and petition, with thanksgiving, they will present their requests to God (Philippians 4:6).

I call those things that be not as though they were in the name of Jesus that those who are going through challenging times are healed, delivered, set free, blessed, and favored and that everything that the enemy meant for evil You are turning around for their good (Romans 4:17).

## Holy Spirit Working of Miracles

For You are El Shaadi, God Almighty, and You can do the impossible.

You are the God of miracles. According to Psalm 77:14, You are the God who performs miracles; You display Your power among the people and through Your people.

I thank You for providing me with the Holy Spirit to work miracles because I hear and believe Your Word by faith in the name of Jesus (Galatians 3:5).

I thank You for a great salvation and that You testify to me and through me by signs and wonders and by various miracles and by the gifts of the Holy Spirit as You will (Hebrews 2:4).

I thank You that as I continue to move forward, there will be a demonstration of a unified and faithful church in truth and love, a display of God's glory to all creation and the world and a reminder to the devil that he is defeated.

I declare in the name of Jesus that utterance may be given to me in the opening of my mouth to make known with boldness the mystery of the Gospel (Ephesians 6:19).

I thank You that the creation of the church through the preaching of the Gospel will display Your presence and glory to proclaim the manifold wisdom of God to the nations and to the rulers and authorities in the heavenly places.

According to Ephesians 3:10–11, "His intent was that now, through the church, the manifold wisdom of God should be made known to the rulers and authorities in the heavenly realms, according to the eternal purpose that He accomplished in Christ Jesus our Lord."

I decree and declare in the name of Jesus that the manifold wisdom of God will be revealed to nations through the kingdom of God in us. For the kingdom of God is within us, and I decree and declare that His presence and glory will be revealed to all humankind through the gifts of the Spirit as He wills, to do mighty exploits and to represent heaven on Earth, in the name of Jesus!

There is nothing too hard for You to do (Jeremiah 32:27). You are able to do exceedingly and abundantly above what we can ask, think, or imagine, according to the power that works in us.

I give You all glory, all honor, and all praise! Thank You, heavenly Father, for the supernatural manifestation of Your presence, power, peace, breakthrough, healing, deliverance, and miracles in my life and the life of others because of Your Holy Word. Thank You for hearing and answering the decrees, declarations, and petitions that I have prayed unto You. So be it unto me according to Your written and Rhema Word. In Jesus's name. Amen!

# CONCLUSION

Father, in the name of Jesus, I thank You for Your Word and for every prayer, decree, and declaration spoken out of the mouths of every individual who reads this book. I declare in the name of Jesus that it fell on good ground today. I thank You that Your Word does not return to You void but accomplishes everything You sent it to do. I thank You that everyone who reads this book will continue to strive to live a life of holiness, one that is acceptable and in complete demonstration of who You are and who of who You are to us. For You are a loving God, and You are a forgiving God. You are also merciful and kind.

I declare in the name of Jesus that as every person who reads this book continues to move forward and be a doer of God's Word, You, Father God, will continue to bless them, increase them, and shower down blessings upon them so that they can shower down blessings upon others in such an amazing way. So be it unto everyone, because you are an amazing God! And I give You glory, honor, and praise, in Jesus's name. Amen.

# RECOMMENDED READINGS AND RESOURCES

Basham, D. 1969. *A Handbook on Holy Spirit Baptism*. New Kensington, PA: Whitaker House.

Cameron, K. 2007. *Why Do I Keep Sinning?* Retrieved from https://www.boundless.org/faith/why-do-i-keep-sinning/.

Coleman, R. E. 1993. *The Master Plan of Evangelism*. Grand Rapids, MI: Baker Publishing Group.

Dixon, O. (2012). *Give me my inheritance*. Los Angeles, CA: Morgan Publishing Company.

Eckhardt, J. (2008). *Prayers that rout demons*. Lake Mary, Florida: Charisma House.

Eckhardt, J. (2010). *Prayers that bring healing*. Lake Mary, Florida: Charisma House.

Hayes, N. (1990). *Know your enemy: how to combat and overcome demonic forces*. Tulsa Oklahoma: Harrison House.

Hayes, N. (2011). *Faith has no feelings*. Tulsa Oklahoma: Harrison House.

Hinn, B. (1990). *Good morning holy spirit*. Nashville, Tennessee: Thomas Nelson Publishers.

Hunter, C. & Hunter, F. (2001). *Handbook for healing*. New Kensington, PA: Whitaker House.

Hunter, C. & Hunter, F. (2012). *How to heal the sick*. New Kensington, PA: Whitaker House.

Nee, W. (1977). *The normal Christian life*. Carol Stream, Illinois: Tyndale House Publishers.

Palmer, L. (2021). *God's purpose for his praise dance ministry: releasing the supernatural to transform, impact, empower and equip*. United States of America: KDP Publishing.

Piper, J. (2000). *Are we to continue in sin that grace might increase?* Retrieved from: https://www.desiringgod.org/messages/are-we-to-continue-in-sin-that-grace-might-increase

Prince, D. (2010). *Prayers & proclamations.* Charlotte, North Carolina: Whitaker House.

Prince, D. (1987). *The holy spirit in you.* Charlotte, North Carolina: Whitaker House.

Prince, D. (2013). *Pulling down strongholds.* Charlotte, North Carolina: Whitaker House.

Socchor, A. (2014). *The root of the problem (part 5).* Retrieved from: https://plainbibleteaching.com/2014/09/01/the-root-of-the-problem-part-5-deception/

Stutts, M. (2019). *Power to transform: radical decrees.* Published in the United States of America.

Timm, C. (2008). *The rules of engagement.* Lake Mary, Florida: Charisma House.

Printed in the United States
by Baker & Taylor Publisher Services